Hidden Treasures
of the Romanovs

SAVING THE ROYAL JEWELS

WILLIAM CLARKE

National
Museums
Scotland

First published in 2009 by
NMS Enterprises Limited – Publishing
a division of NMS Enterprises Limited
National Museums Scotland
Chambers Street
Edinburgh EH1 1JF

www.nms.ac.uk

ISBN: 978-1-905267-25-5

British Library Cataloguing in Publication Data
A catalogue record for this book
is available from the British Library.

ISBN: 978 1 905267 25 5

Cover design by Mark Blackadder.

IMAGE CREDITS FOR COVER:

Background: View of the Nevsky Prospect, *c.*1900
(source: Library of Congress).

Foreground (left): The Vladimir Tiara, owned by the
Grand Duchess Maria Pavlovna of Russia (Grand
Duchess Vladimir), now owned by HM Queen
Elizabeth II (source: Peter Macdiarmid/Getty Images
News/Getty Images).

Foreground (right): The Grand Duchess Maria
Pavlovna wearing the tiara (source: Wartski London).

Printed by Kripps – a Euradius company –
in The Netherlands.

For a full listing of NMS Enterprises Limited –
Publishing titles and related merchandise:

shop.nms.ac.uk

CONTENTS

IMAGE AND TEXT CREDITS

The following listings contain acknowledgements for use of source material and photographs within this publication. No reproduction of material in copyright is permitted without prior contact with the publisher or with original sources.

IMAGE ACKNOWLEDGEMENTS AND PERMISSIONS

MARTIN ANDERSON

© for page 88; and art section pages 8(x2)

WILLIAM CLARKE

Source for page 11

GETTY IMAGES®
101 Bayham Street
London NW1 OAG
www.gettyimages.com

© for pages xvii (Popperfoto/Getty Images), 14 (Popperfoto/Getty Images), 72 (Hulton Archive/ Getty Images), 108 (Hulton Archive/Topical Press Agency/ Getty Images); cover (tiara) and art section page 16 (Peter Macdiarmid/ Getty Images News/Getty Images)

ILLUSTRATED LONDON NEWS
Images managed by
Mary Evans Picture Library
59 Tranquil Vale
Blackheath, London SE3 OBS
www.ilnpictures.co.uk

Source for pages 22, 38, 54; and art section pages 2, 6(x2), 9(x2), 10(x2), 11(x4), 12(x2), 13(x5)

LIBRARY OF CONGRESS
(Prints and Photographs Division)
Washington DC 20540, USA
http://hdl.loc.gov/loc.pnp/pp.print

Source for cover (background); pages 28, 45; and art section pages 4(x3), 5(x3), 8(x3), 10(x1), 11(x3), 12(x1), 13(x2), 14(x3), 15(x4)
see George Grantham Bain Collection (Library of Congress)

NATIONAL MUSEUMS SCOTLAND
Chambers Street
Edinburgh EH1 1JF
www.nms.ac.uk

© Trustees of the National Museums Scotland for art section page 5

NATIONAL PORTRAIT GALLERY
St Martin's Place
London WC2H OHE
www.npg.org.uk

© for art section pages 4, 10

ONE MAN IN HIS TIME
Serge Obolensky

(© 1960 published by Hutchinson. Reprinted by kind permission of The Random House Group Ltd)

Source for page 81

ROYAL SCOTS DRAGOON GUARDS [CARABINIERS AND GREYS]

© for art section page 3

SOTHEBY'S
34-35 New Bond Street
London W1A 2AA
www.sothebys.com

© for art section page 1
(Cecil Beaton, 1904-1980; 'Albert Stopford' courtesy of the Cecil Beaton Studio Archive at Sotheby's)

THE WAR ILLUSTRATED
Album Deluxe
edited by J. A. Hammerton
(London: The Amalgamated Press Ltd, 1915 and 16)
vol. I (*The First Phase*), vol. II (*The Winter Campaign*), vol. IV (*The Summer Campaign 1915*), vol. V (*The Winter Campaign 1915-16*)
Source for page 42 (x2); and art section pages 6(x2), 7(x3), 9

WARTSKI, LONDON
14 Grafton Street
London W15 4DE

© for cover (picture of Grand Duchess Maria Pavlovna) and art section page 16(x2)

TEXT ACKNOWLEDGEMENTS AND PERMISSIONS

MARGARET ALLEN
for assistance in the research of Sicilian authors.

ARCHIVES (MISCELLANEOUS)
for assistance in aspects of research in this book:

Family Records Centre, London
for information relating to the family of Rev. Frederick Manners Stopford.
Heinemann (Publishers) Archives
for information relating to the original publication of *The Russian Diary of an Englishman in Petrograd, 1915-1917* [1919].
HSBC Group Archives
for information relating to the Appendix.
Lambeth Palace Archives
for information relating to the family of Rev. Frederick Manners Stopford.

BRITISH LIBRARY NEWSPAPERS ARCHIVE
for the reproduction of extracts from *John Bull* journal from 20 July 1918 and 27 July 1918.

CAMBRIDGE UNIVERSITY PRESS
for permission to reproduce extracts from *The Letters of D. H. Lawrence*, vols III, IV and V, edited by James T. Boulton, *et al.* (reproduced by permission of Pollinger Limited, the Estate of Frieda Lawrence Ravagli and Cambridge University Press, © The Estate of Frieda Lawrence Ravagli 1979, 1981, 1984, 1987, 1989, 1991, 1993).

CARTIER, PARIS
for access to information relating to the jewels of the Grand Duchess Maria Pavlovna.

CONSTABLE AND ROBINSON
for permission to reproduce an extract from Barbara Tuchman: *The Guns of August – August 1914* (© 1962, by kind permission of the publisher).

DANCE BOOKS LTD
for permission to reproduce extracts from Mathilde Kschessinka: *Dancing in Petersburg* (for © details contact Dancing Books Ltd).

DAVID HIGHAM ASSOCIATES
for permission to reproduce extracts from Tamara Karsavina: *Theatre Street* (© 1930 William Heinemann).

HRH PRINCESS ELIZABETH OF YUGOSLAVIA
for assistance in the research of the jewels of Grand Duchess Maria Pavlovna; and for permission to reproduce extracts from the letters of Grand Duchess Maria Pavlovna to Alexander Ouchakoff (1914-20); a letter dated 15 June 1920 from Grand Duchess Maria Pavlovna to Albert Stopford; and the Diary of Princess Olga [Maria Pavlovna's grand-daughter] (reprinted by kind permission).

COUNT HANS VEIT TOERRING-JETTENBACH
for interview and assistance in the research of the jewels of Grand Duchess Maria Pavlovna.

GRETCHEN HASKIN
with grateful thanks for access to a private memorandum and additional support in research.

HRH PRINCESS HELENE OF HABSBURG
for interview and assistance in the research of the jewels of Grand Duchess Maria Pavlovna.

HELEN MARX BOOKS, NEW YORK
for permission to reproduce extracts from Felix Youssoupoff: *Lost Splendour* (originally published in 1953; © reprinted by kind permission of Helen Marx Books, New York).

MARY HUGHES (*neé* STOPFORD), ANGELA PRICE (*neé* STOPFORD) AND NIGEL PRICE
for interview and assistance in the research of John Stopford and Albert Henry Stopford.

LEEDS RUSSIAN ARCHIVE (BROTHERTON LIBRARY) UNIVERSITY OF LEEDS
for permission to reproduce extracts from the Lady Muriel Paget Papers. Leeds Russian Archive MS.1405. Leeds University Library).

HAROLD LINDES
for permission to use information from the memorandum written by Alexei Pilatsky.

LYNN C. FRANKLIN ASSOCIATES LTD
for permission to reproduce extracts from Edvard Radzinsky: *Rasputin* (from *The Rasputin File* by Edvard Radzinsky, originally published in the US by Doubleday, Copyright © 2000 by Edvard Radzinsky, all rights reserved).

HRH PRINCE MICHAEL OF KENT
for interview and research about HRH Princess Marina, the grand-daughter of Grand Duchess Maria Pavlovna, the jewels of Grand Duchess Maria Pavlovna and the layout of the Vladimir Palace.

HENRY POOLE
for permission to reproduce extracts from the papers of General Frederick Poole.

THE NATIONAL ARCHIVES
for the reproduction of extracts from the following sources:
FO 371, FO 371/3326 and FO 371/3398, FO 395/184;
HO 45/11026/413565 and HO 140/346;
WO 339/55793 and WO 372/19;
CRIM 4/1403.

NEW YORK PUBLIC LIBRARY FOR THE PERFORMING ARTS
for information relating to the *Ballets Russes* (with thanks to the Dance Division, Lincoln Centre, New York).

NORTHAMPTONSHIRE RECORD OFFICE
for permission to reproduce letters from Francis Stopford to Canon Luckock (2 April 1912 [328p/23/1] and 18 August 1912 [328p/23/2]).

OFFICE DE TOURISME CONTREXEVILLE, FRANCE
for assistance in the research of Grand Duchess Maria Pavlovna and her time in Contrexeville.

GIOVANNI PANARELLO
for assistance in the research of Albert Stopford's time in Taormina.

QUATTROSOLI
for permission to reproduce extract from Filippo Calandruccio: *Beehive: oltre un secolo di attività turistica a Taormina* (© 1993, contact Quattrosoli).

THE RANDOM HOUSE GROUP
for permission to reproduce extracts from Richard Pipes: *The Russian Revolution* (© 1990 published by Harvill. Reprinted by kind permission of The Random House Group Ltd); and Serge Obolensky: *One Man in His Time* (© 1960 published by Hutchinson. Reprinted by kind permission of The Random House Group Ltd).

ROYAL OPERA HOUSE
for permission to reproduce extracts from Charles Neilson Gattey: 'Lady de Grey and the Garden's Golden Age', published in Spring 1992 issue of the Royal Opera House magazine *About the House* (for © contact the Royal Opera House).

SCOTS GUARDS ARCHIVE
for access to correspondence from Frank Cousins to his sister, in Frank C. Cousins Collection, Scots Guards Archive, Wellington Barracks, London.

SERVICE CENTRALE DES CIMETIERES, PARIS
for assistance in the research of Albert Stopford's burial details.

STATE ARCHIVES OF THE RUSSIAN FEDERATION, MOSCOW, RUSSIA
for access to the correspondence between Albert Henry Stopford and Grand Duchess Maria Pavlovna, Sr. Fond 655.

THAMES & HUDSON
for permission to reproduce extracts from Hans Nadelhoffer: *Cartier: Jewelers Extraordinary* (© 1984 Hans Nadelhoffer. Reprinted by kind permission of Thames & Hudson Ltd, London).

DR IDRIS TRAYLOR
for assistance in the layout of the Vladimir Palace and additional support in research.

UNIVERSITY COLLEGE, OXFORD
for assistance in the research of Eric Hamilton.

IAN VORRES
for permission to reproduce extracts from: Ian Vorres: *The Last Grand Duchess* (© Ian Vorres).

WARTSKI'S ARCHIVES, LONDON (FABERGÉ ACCOUNTS)
for access to and permission to reproduce extracts from the accounts of Fabergé, 1900s. (Wartski's Archives, 14 Grafton Street, London).

GEOFFREY MUNN, WARTSKI
for assistance in research on the subject of tiaras and information on Wartski's historical connection with Romanov jewels.

WEIDENFELD AND NICHOLSON (THE ORION PUBLISHING GROUP)
for permission to reproduce extract from Duff Cooper and edited by John Julian Norwich: *The Duff Cooper Diaries* (© 2006 Weidenfeld and Nicholson, an imprint of The Orion Publishing Group, London).

THE WINTERTHUR LIBRARY, DELAWARE, USA
for permission to reproduce extracts from May Bourne Strassburger Papers (Box 1 Folders 8-9) (Courtesy, The Winterthur Library: Joseph Downs Collection of Manuscripts and Printed Ephemera).

CHRISTOPHER WYLD
for permission to reproduce extracts from the memoir of Eric Hamilton (reprinted by kind permission).

ACKNOWLEDGEMENTS

I HAVE acknowledged individual text sources in the references to each chapter and on pages V-VI and am indebted to all those who have guided, advised or provided me with invaluable information. Some individuals provided me with similar help for an earlier book of mine, *The Lost Fortune of the Tsars* (1994/2007), where I briefly referred to Albert Stopford's exploits. Two people in particular – Gretchen Haskin in San Francisco and Idris Traylor in Texas – not only offered their own knowledge and contacts freely, but have been a constant support throughout my researches.

In assessing the jewels Stopford rescued and their sharing out among Grand Duchess Maria's royal descendants, I am deeply indebted to Count Hans Veit Toerring-Jettenbach in Munich whose assistance was unstinting. So too was that of his cousin HRH Princess Elizabeth of Yugloslavia in Belgrade, who provided me with photographs of Maria's jewels for reference and copies of Maria's private correspondence between 1914 and 1920. I am similarly indebted to their cousin, HRH Prince Michael of Kent, for his own help concerning Maria's jewels, and for his intimate knowledge of Maria's Vladimir Palace in St Petersburg.

John Stopford's family – Mary Hughes (*née* Stopford), Angela Price (*née* Stopford) and Nigel Price – provided invaluable information about Albert Stopford's rescue of the jewels and his subsequent life in Paris, as well as sharing details with me about Albert's possessions. I greatly benefited from their own private investigations.

Stopford's life in Sicily was initially revealed through his correspondence with D. H. Lawrence and a local interview with a Rome newspaper – both of which emerged from the Internet. In the follow-up detection I was greatly helped by the local Italian knowledge and investigative instincts of a former colleague of mine on *The Times*, the financial journalist and author Margaret Allen. Her familiarity with Sicilian authors was invaluable to this project.

I am particularly grateful to Cartier in Paris for allowing me, with the willing consent of Grand Duchess Maria's descendants, to examine their dealings with Maria Pavlovna and their valuation of certain of her jewels undertaken after her death in 1920. In London, I must thank Geoffrey Munn at Wartski jewellers for sharing with me his unique knowledge of tiaras and his firm's historical connection with Romanov jewels. Wartski also gave me permission to examine the London archives of Fabergé, now in their possession.

Thanks are also due to the Dance Division of New York Public Libraries; the Family Records Centre in London, Northamptonshire Record Office; State Archives of the Russian Federation; University College, Oxford; Leeds Russian Archives (Brotherton Library); The National Archives; British Library Newspaper Archives; the Scots Guards Archives; Heinemann Archives; Office de Tourisme Contrexeville, France; The Winterthur Library, USA; Service Centrale des Cimetieres, Paris; HSBC Group Archives – and to all publishers who permitted me to use extracts of their published work (see the acknowledgements on pages V-VI).

Members of my own family have once again assisted me in some of the research. My daughter Deborah in France explored the intricacies of French officialdom in discovering Stopford's death and burial in Paris, as well as translating all of Maria Pavlovna's French correspondence. My daughter Pamela and her friend Gabriella Frederiksen coped with the Italian translations. My wife Faith has again shared in much of the research, some of the travel, and provided continuing advice on the inevitable drafts that flow through the house.

William Clarke

INTRODUCTION

B EYOND the end of the Metro line, south of Paris, lies the cemetery of Bagneux. It was here in 1900 that the body of Oscar Wilde was originally buried, after he had been abandoned, virtually destitute, by most of his London friends. Bagneux is that kind of place, with rows upon rows of graves, somewhat desolate, in an outer suburb. Little wonder then that Wilde's real friends finally paid for his removal to the more fashionable cemetery at Père Lachaise.

No such elevation was to follow for the remains of another London exile, a contemporary of Wilde, the Honorable Albert Henry Stopford, who is also buried at Bagneux. His present place of rest can no longer be identified, as his remains were removed to the communal section of the cemetery thirty years after his interment in 1939 – a forgotten man in a foreign land.

In his time, however, Albert Stopford had delivered private messages from George V to Nicholas II, the last Russian Tsar. He counted Nijinsky, Tamara Karsavina and Anna Pavlova from the *Ballet Russes* among his friends. And during the months leading up to the October/November Revolution, Stopford was right in very storm-centre, avoiding machine-gun fire and sabre attacks as he moved through the dangerous streets of Petrograd to rescue treasured artefacts on behalf of the Romanov family. It is because of Stopford that on special occasions to this day Her Majesty Queen Elizabeth II wears a tiara saved from the clutches of the Bolsheviks.

But in less than nine months during the last year of the First World War, Albert Stopford went from being a member of the highest echelons of British and Russian society, the eyes and ears of both the War Office and the British Ambassador in St Petersburg, to being shunned by all but a few of his staunchest friends. Only weeks after the end of the war on 11 November 1918, a war in which he had carved out such a special, almost heroic, niche for himself, he was sentenced to twelve months' hard labour at the Old Bailey. On his release from Wormwood Scrubs, Albert Stopford was rarely seen in London again.

Stopford had moved with ease among the top families of the London and Paris *belle époque*. Like so many of his society friends, he had lived a leisurely life at a time when European wealth was at its peak and extravagance its very watchword. But as a typical Edwardian man about town, Stopford was not the only member of that prosperous era to be tested in a way no one could have contemplated before 1914. His friends in London, Paris and St Petersburg would now face the bloodshed and turmoil of the First World War in vastly different ways.

The *belle époque* had merged seamlessly into Edwardian Britain as Paris and London vied in fashion, taste and extravagance. Tsarist Russia too – or at least its extended Romanov family and narrow cultural élite based in St Petersburg – was also beginning to leave its mark. Throughout the previous century, wealth, both old and new, had accumulated in the hands of a privileged few, and the theatres, shops and luxury hotels of Paris, London and St Petersburg stood as testimony to the ease with which it could be spent.

As the 19th century reached its conclusion, France's humiliation at the hands of Otto von Bismark was already fading, and the theatres, opera houses and dance halls of Paris thronged with the well-to-do. In Britain the Victorian era had provided a sense of self-confidence that was soon to burst into the exuberance of the Edwardians.

Meanwhile, in far-off St Petersburg Russia's cultural spirit had also begun to burn very bright. But as the social élite enjoyed the pleasures of the Imperial ballet and the finest works of Peter Karl Fabergé, political unrest and bloody acts of terrorism were never far from the surface.

Stopford, and the friends he slowly accumulated throughout Europe's capitals, had been brought up in a comfortable monarchical society, where status and wealth opened the right doors. Accepted patterns of behaviour were considered *de rigeur*. But as the twentieth century dawned, less restraint was being applied to taste and fashion. Stopford's circle of friends and acquaintances were major participants in a European society that was edging ever closer to the abyss of war and revolution. Virtually all of them were connected in some way with reigning monarchs throughout Europe, and most had interest in or involvement with Tsarist Russia.

Pride of place in this book's cast of characters must go to the likes of Lady Constance Gladys Herbert of London, whose grandmother hailed from one of the oldest aristocratic families in Russia. Sharing the limelight with Lady Gladys is the Grand Duchess Maria Pavlovna of St Petersburg, the sister-in-law of Tsar Alexander III and aunt of Nicholas II. Both ladies were leading players in the cutural life of their countries and shared an unerring instinct for the bohemian.

From the younger members of the cast Prince Felix Yusupov is also a main player, an extravagant character who hailed from the richest family in Russia. Likewise Grand Duke Dmitri Pavlovich, who was implicated with Yusupov in the murder of Rasputin before both men were sent into exile. And adding his own voice to the cast is Prince Serge Obolensky, whose exploits in the glittering world of Edwardian London probably astounded himself as much as they did his friends.

All these characters met Albert Stopford at key moments in his life, and came to regard him as a close friend, a man for all occasions. But in their own way, they provided the catalyst that brought the Englishman closer to his own destiny, as they celebrated their wealth and privilege, giving little thought to the ephemeral nature of the society that created it.

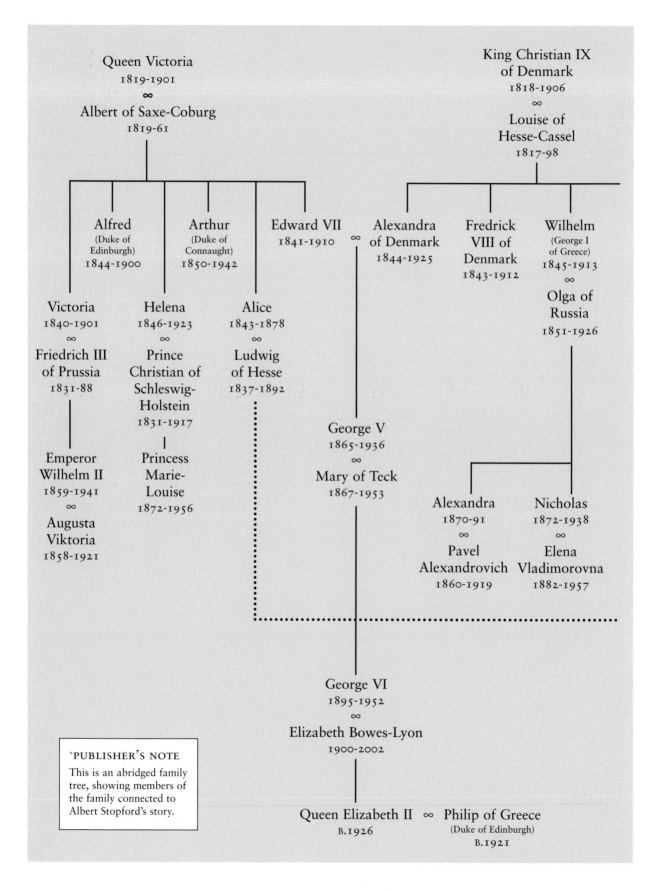

Queen Victoria
1819-1901
∞
Albert of Saxe-Coburg
1819-61

King Christian IX
of Denmark
1818-1906
∞
Louise of
Hesse-Cassel
1817-98

Alfred
(Duke of
Edinburgh)
1844-1900

Arthur
(Duke of
Connaught)
1850-1942

Edward VII
1841-1910   ∞

Alexandra
of Denmark
1844-1925

Fredrick
VIII of
Denmark
1843-1912

Wilhelm
(George I
of Greece)
1845-1913
∞
Olga of
Russia
1851-1926

Victoria
1840-1901
∞
Friedrich III
of Prussia
1831-88

Helena
1846-1923
∞
Prince
Christian of
Schleswig-
Holstein
1831-1917

Alice
1843-1878
∞
Ludwig
of Hesse
1837-1892

Emperor
Wilhelm II
1859-1941
∞
Augusta
Viktoria
1858-1921

Princess
Marie-
Louise
1872-1956

George V
1865-1936
∞
Mary of Teck
1867-1953

Alexandra
1870-91
∞
Pavel
Alexandrovich
1860-1919

Nicholas
1872-1938
∞
Elena
Vladimorovna
1882-1957

George VI
1895-1952
∞
Elizabeth Bowes-Lyon
1900-2002

*PUBLISHER'S NOTE
This is an abridged family
tree, showing members of
the family connected to
Albert Stopford's story.

Queen Elizabeth II   ∞   Philip of Greece
B.1926   (Duke of Edinburgh)
                            B.1921

Family Tree*

THE ROYAL FAMILIES OF EUROPE

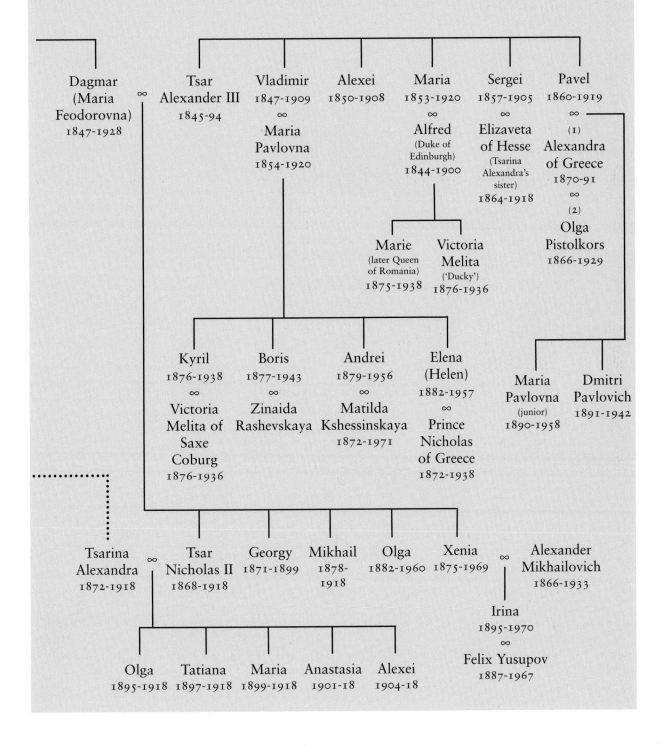

Dagmar (Maria Feodorovna) 1847-1928

∞

Tsar Alexander III 1845-94

Vladimir 1847-1909
∞
Maria Pavlovna 1854-1920

Alexei 1850-1908

Maria 1853-1920
∞
Alfred (Duke of Edinburgh) 1844-1900

Sergei 1857-1905
∞
Elizaveta of Hesse (Tsarina Alexandra's sister) 1864-1918

Pavel 1860-1919
∞
(1)
Alexandra of Greece 1870-91
∞
(2)
Olga Pistolkors 1866-1929

Marie (later Queen of Romania) 1875-1938

Victoria Melita ('Ducky') 1876-1936

Kyril 1876-1938
∞
Victoria Melita of Saxe Coburg 1876-1936

Boris 1877-1943
∞
Zinaida Rashevskaya

Andrei 1879-1956
∞
Matilda Kshessinskaya 1872-1971

Elena (Helen) 1882-1957
∞
Prince Nicholas of Greece 1872-1938

Maria Pavlovna (junior) 1890-1958

Dmitri Pavlovich 1891-1942

Tsarina Alexandra 1872-1918

∞

Tsar Nicholas II 1868-1918

Georgy 1871-1899

Mikhail 1878-1918

Olga 1882-1960

Xenia 1875-1969

∞

Alexander Mikhailovich 1866-1933

Irina 1895-1970
∞
Felix Yusupov 1887-1967

Olga 1895-1918

Tatiana 1897-1918

Maria 1899-1918

Anastasia 1901-18

Alexei 1904-18

for Faith

CORONATION DAY, 1911

The Royal procession at Westminster, London, as
the crowds attend the coronation of King George V
on 22 June 1911.

(© Popperfoto/Getty Images)

CHAPTER ONE

Coronation Gala
1911

THE Edwardian era, the first decade of the twentieth century, has in retrospect been viewed as a period of gaiety and good living, a reflection of the monarch himself. Even in his last days, during the late spring of 1910, Edward VII was still struggling with what a biographer described as his restless energy. Having just returned from Biarritz after a rough Channel crossing, he was attending a performance of *Rigoletto* at Covent Garden only two hours later. And though suffering from a bout of bronchitis, he insisted on going back to see it again. The wind and rain at Sandringham that weekend, combined with Edward's determination to fulfil all his duties the following week, hardly helped. Despite all his efforts to continue as normal, the King's heart began to fail and he could breathe only with great difficulty. The end was near. The final coherent words of Edward VII on the evening of 6 May were to express delight that his horse Witch of Air had won the 4.15 at Kempton Park.

The Edwardian era perhaps reached its zenith a full year after the King's death, during the week-long celebration of George V's coronation on 22 June 1911, when London's summer season was given over to any conceivable excuse for extravagance and *joie de vivre*.

One society lady in particular, Lady Constance Gladys de Grey, the Marchioness of Ripon,[1] had more cause for satisfaction than most that week. Twice within five days she had looked down at the spectacle before her from her regular box at the Royal Opera House, with her daughter Lady Juliet Duff by her side. On the night before the coronation itself, Lady Gladys watched the triumphant first night success of Sergei Diaghilev's *Ballets Russes* in its inaugural London season. Now, four days after the coronation, she was back again for a special gala performance in the presence of the newly-crowned King George V and Queen Mary.

Both events were down to the superb organisational skills of Lady Gladys. For well over a decade she had not only moulded the Royal Opera House at Covent Garden in the form of her own hopes and aspirations, but also found time to maintain her favourable

reputation as one of the most gracious hostesses of the Edwardian era. On that very special Coronation Gala evening at Covent Garden, the house was crowded with many of her society friends, including the Royal family, as well as artists she had met and supported in the literary and cultural circles of London, Paris and St Petersburg.

Lady Gladys's triumph in 1911 was by no means her first contribution to the arts in London. She had already established her credentials by advising and supporting the impresario Sir Augustus Harris in his new and enterprising operatic ventures in the capital. She also had close links with Covent Garden, where a family relation, Harry Higgins, was for many years co-manager. Since the days of popular singers such as Jenny Lind and Adelina Patti, Covent Garden had lost its ability to put on well-staged productions and to attract the world's finest entertainers. It now had rivals elsewhere in London, especially at Drury Lane. Lady Gladys and fellow members of the so-called 'Marlborough House Set',[2] such as Lady Charles Beresford, were convinced that Harris's successes could and should be transferred to their rightful home at Covent Garden, and between them they undertook to secure regular subscriptions for individual boxes in the theatre. This became the turning point in Covent Garden's overdue revival, supported by a Grand Opera Syndicate hastily created on Harris's death in 1896 by Lady Gladys's husband Lord Frederick de Grey,[3] and several of Harris's friends. Harry Higgins became chairman, while Lord Frederick stood as a director.[4]

Evidence of Lady Gladys's influence in the arts had been amply demonstrated back in 1889 when she successfully launched the London career of the Australian singer Nellie Melba at the Royal Opera House. They first met in Paris where Lady Gladys kept an apartment. Melba described the occasion, as well as her general impression of her patron, in her memoirs:

> She was a grande dame, a type of aristocracy of which London can boast of only too few today. There was an instinctive nobility about everything she did or said. I shall never forget the first time that I met her, before I had returned to London. It was in the Hotel Scribe in Paris, in the morning, and the spring sunshine was drifting into her apartment, lighting up the gorgeous green foulard dress which she was wearing. She was sitting at her writing table, and as she turned round the sun illuminated her lovely profile, making me catch my breath with the beauty of it.
>
> It was Gladys who gave me my first London party; that is to say, the first party to which I went after I became a somebody. I was thrilled by the very thought of going to a party, but far more thrilled after I had been sitting in her beautiful salon in Bruton Street for about ten minutes. Never shall I forget the succession of women who

drifted into that room – the Duchess of Leinster, robed in white satin with marvellous sapphires round her neck, holding her head like a Queen; Lady Dudley, with her lovely turquoises, so numerous that they seemed to cover her from her head to her knees; and Lady Warwick, then at the height of her beauty; the old Duchess of Devonshire, making somewhat pointed comments on those around her, the brilliant Duchess of Sutherland, Lady Cynthia Graham, Lady Helen Vincent, and many others.

Lady Gladys de Grey was among the last of the women who have been capable of holding a salon, with all that that word implies. She did not confine her hospitality to one class alone, she invited every type, and by some magic of personality, seemed to blend them all into a harmonious whole.[5]

Melba's gratitude to Lady Gladys is understandable. The singer had already been successfully introduced to a Parisian audience, but an earlier London debut had been disappointing. Lady Gladys, having previously heard Melba sing in Brussels, met with her in Paris and offered some assistance. With such determined backing, Melba's second appearance thirteen months later at Covent Garden was a critical success, thanks to her patron's ability to ensure the attendance of the cream of society. Lady Gladys also arranged for Melba to sing at Windsor Castle for Queen Victoria and Empress Augusta Viktoria, wife of the Queen's grandson Kaiser Wilhelm II.

Lady Gladys de Grey was born Constance Gladys (or Gwladys) Herbert. She had Russian blood in her veins inherited from her grandmother Catherine Worontzof, daughter of Count Simon Worontzof, a former Russian Ambassador in London. She was likewise well connected through her father Sydney Herbert, who had been Britain's Foreign Secretary during the Crimean War.

As a young debutante noted for her beauty and elegance, she quickly attracted attention, a quality that continued throughout her life as she graced her own salons in Paris and London. One of the first to notice her was Oscar Wilde's mother Speranza who entertained fleeting hopes that Gladys might marry her son.[6] By 1878, however, Gladys had demonstrated that she preferred the peerage to a more bohemian lifestyle by marrying the Earl of Lonsdale. Nonetheless she remained one of Oscar Wilde's 'beautiful people' and was frequently invited to his residence at Thames House just off the Strand.

After the unexpected early death of the Earl of Lonsdale in 1882, Gladys married Lord de Grey in 1885, described in *The Tatler* as one of the best shots in the land.[7] Soon the couple were hosting some of the most popular parties in London at their house in Bruton Street, round the corner from Berkeley Square. Oscar Wilde was a regular guest and remained a close friend of the de Greys, dedicating the

published version of his play *A Woman of No Importance* to Lady Gladys. And it was at one of her lively parties that Wilde greeted a newcomer with the well known put-down: 'Oh, I'm so glad you've come. There are a hundred things I want not to say to you.'[8]

Some of the leading performers at Covent Garden – such as Enrico Caruso, Nellie Melba and the Polish de Reske brothers, Edouard and Jean – were also regular guests at Bruton Street. They usually required little encouragement to sing or even parody their own performances.[9]

By 1911 Lady Gladys's patronage for music, opera and ballet had extended to the exciting and relatively new *Ballets Russes*. Her interest may have been inspired by her Russian connections, but no one recognised her contribution more than the man in charge of the company, Sergei Pavlovich Diaghilev. In an article in *The Observer* many years later, Diaghilev enthused about Lady Gladys and how she championed the cause of the *Ballets Russes* and Covent Garden.[10]

Having been overwhelmed two years earlier by the success of the *Ballets Russes* in Paris, Lady Gladys set out to attract the remarkable Russian company to London. Her original plan to bring them to Covent Garden in 1910 was delayed due to the sudden death of King Edward. But her close connections at court, especially with the newly widowed Queen Alexandra, made it easier to persuade the Palace to make Diaghilev's company a major part of the forthcoming coronation festivities.

At the turn of the twentieth century the Russian Imperial Ballet, based at the Mariinsky Theatre in St Petersburg, had been poised for a remarkable transformation. All the principal players who were to take the West by storm over the next decade were either already employed by the Mariinsky or just emerging from its ballet school. Sergei Diaghilev had taken over the Theatre's publications, Michel Fokine made his debut in 1898, Anna Pavlova and Tamara Karsavina were in their later years at the school, and the prodigy Vaslav Nijinsky had just joined.[11] It was to be another ten years before the group finally gained international recognition through the combined enterprise of Sergei Diaghilev and Gabriel Astruc, the French impresario based at Le Chatelet Theatre in Paris.[12]

Ballets Russes was also provided with essential patronage at home by Tsar Nicholas II's uncle, Grand Duke Vladimir Alexandrovich and his wife Grand Duchess Maria Pavlovna. Like the de Greys in London, Vladimir's family were leading lights of the upper class in St Petersburg.

In the first decade of the twentieth century, oblivious to the spectre of war looming on the horizon, St Petersburg's high society was in full swing. The court, however, had grown to accept that their Tsarina, Alexandra Feodorovna, was unwilling, or perhaps unable, to play

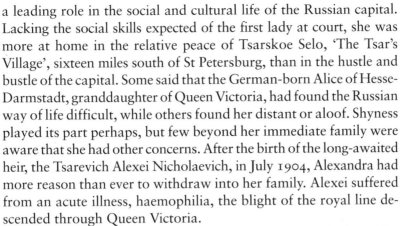

a leading role in the social and cultural life of the Russian capital. Lacking the social skills expected of the first lady at court, she was more at home in the relative peace of Tsarskoe Selo, 'The Tsar's Village', sixteen miles south of St Petersburg, than in the hustle and bustle of the capital. Some said that the German-born Alice of Hesse-Darmstadt, granddaughter of Queen Victoria, had found the Russian way of life difficult, while others found her distant or aloof. Shyness played its part perhaps, but few beyond her immediate family were aware that she had other concerns. After the birth of the long-awaited heir, the Tsarevich Alexei Nicholaevich, in July 1904, Alexandra had more reason than ever to withdraw into her family. Alexei suffered from an acute illness, haemophilia, the blight of the royal line descended through Queen Victoria.

Whatever her reasons, Alexandra's reluctance to involve herself in social matters at court created a vacancy that was willingly filled by individuals such as Nicholas's mother, the Danish-born Dowager Empress Maria Feodorovna (widow of Tsar Alexander III), and his aunt Maria Pavlovna. Between them they organised their own court, with its seemingly endless round of receptions, dances and *soirées*, and lent their support to cultural ventures, such as the *Ballets Russes*.

Diaghilev's company gave its first international performance in Paris on 19 May 1909 and made an immediate impact on all who saw it. Further European venues followed and plans were quickly set in place for a second season in the French capital. Lady Gladys had already enjoyed a performance by the Russian company during a visit to the Empress Maria Feodorovna in St Petersburg and had been present for its huge success in Paris. Lady Juliet Duff had also watched them dance in Monte Carlo, and their shared enthusiasm prompted Lady Gladys to write to Diaghilev:

> I thought I had experienced everything life could give, but you have brought a new joy into my life – the greatest and last – and you must come to London for King Edward would simply adore your productions.[13]

Despite the King's death in 1910 Lady Gladys pursued her plan to arrange a season at Covent Garden. It was not that London had been denied the chance to see individual dancers from the Russian ballet before, for the prima ballerina Anna Pavlova had already appeared in solo dances at the Palace Theatre; but Lady Gladys had something more special in mind – a season of the full Diaghilev *Ballets Russes* at Covent Garden. The first night would be arranged for the eve of Coronation Day, with a special gala in the presence of the newly crowned King and Queen a few days later.

The *Ballets Russes* gave its first performance, choreographed by Michel Fokine, in London at the Royal Opera House, Covent Garden on 21 June 1911, introducing excerpts from *Le Pavillon d'Armide* featuring Nijinsky and Tamara Karsavina, *Carnaval* with Nijinsky, as well as *Prince Igor* and *Paganini*. It was Nijinsky's first appearance in London and the reception was unprecedented.

As Coronation Day dawned, the London critics filled the newspapers with their superlatives. With *The Times* describing the choreography as amongst the best ever witnessed, even Diaghilev, a cynic by nature, had to admit it had been a great success.[14]

It was little wonder then that Lady Gladys's Coronation Gala, set to follow on Monday 26 June, became an overnight 'must' for London society. Applications for tickets flooded in to fill Covent Garden twenty times over. With one-third reserved for the King's guests, rumours circulated that offers of up to £1000 (c.£57,000 today) had been made for the remaining individual boxes. Cheaper boxes at eight guineas were snapped up for a hundred, with offers of five hundred eventually having to be turned down. Even the cheaper seats were in much demand. The first person to join the gallery queue, much to the astonishment of the policeman on duty, was wearing formal court dress, and those who followed were equally resplendent in evening attire.

On the night, as though to match the splendour of the audience, the house was decorated with 100,000 roses, prompting Diaghilev to comment that there were almost as many roses in the house as maharajahs. The Royal box in the centre of the grand tier was surrounded by a frieze of gold, white and mauve orchids. The glittering audience, in the presence of the King and Queen – George in his admiral's uniform, Mary in rose-pink embroidered with jewels, with the huge Cullinan diamond and Star of Africa on her bodice – were entertained by operatic contributions from Nellie Melba and John McCormack, as well as excerpts from the new Diaghilev repertoire. The Russian Empress Maria Feodorovna was also present in the Royal box as a guest of her sister Alexandra, the Queen Mother.

Of all the performances presented during that first full Russian season at Covent Garden, one in particular seized the imagination of the public – Nijinsky in *La Spectre de la Rose*. His famous exit from the centre of the stage, when he appeared to fly into the air and remain motionless for a moment before disappearing through the windows into the summer night, astonished the audience. At the company's earlier performance in Monte Carlo, the same leap was said to have produced such a spontaneous burst of loud and continuous applause that the orchestra was unable to finish the music. On the stage at Covent Garden, Nijinsky's leap was set to become the stuff of legend.

Prima ballerina Tamara Karsavina, who danced with Nijinsky in *La Spectre* during that triumphant London season, later tried to

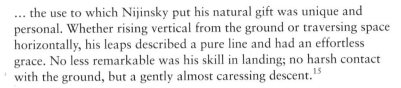

explain where his genius lay. His 'elevation', as she liked to call it, could be put down quite simply to the unusual strength and development of his thighs and Achilles tendons:

> ... the use to which Nijinsky put his natural gift was unique and personal. Whether rising vertical from the ground or traversing space horizontally, his leaps described a pure line and had an effortless grace. No less remarkable was his skill in landing; no harsh contact with the ground, but a gently almost caressing descent.[15]

Nijinsky himself, when asked how he managed to stay in the air, explained it in rather more prosaic terms: 'No, no. It is not difficult. You have just got to go up and then pause a little up there.'[16]

Karsavina was already dancing the lead in five-act ballets when she first met Nijinsky. He was in his final year at the ballet school:

> ... in the crowd of other boys, now carrying the train of the Queen, now one of the tormenting spirits in the *Vision of Raymonde*, there moved, unnoticed, the Eighth Wonder of the World. ... 'Who is this,' I asked. His master replied, 'It is Nijinsky, the little devil never comes down'.[17]

Tamara Karsavina's father had been first dancer with the Imperial Mariinsky Theatre and teacher at the Imperial Ballet School, and insisted that his daughter took dancing lessons for years before performing on stage. Once there, however, her progress under the wing of Diaghilev was assured. Not long after her triumphs in Paris and London, she paid fulsome tribute to their London sponsor Lady Gladys de Grey. Following a performance of *Giselle* at the Mariinsky Theatre in St Petersburg, Empress Maria Feodorovna, enjoying the spectacle from the Imperial box, sent for the ballerina. 'I am told you have had a great success in England,' the Empress said to her. Karsavina 'saw at once that [Lady Gladys] had been instrumental in bringing about this favour and thanked her on [their] next meeting. "Oh yes," [Lady Gladys] said with her sweet smile, "I took down all your photos to Sandringham for the Empress to see".'[18]

Diana Cooper, a young socialite still under her mother's eagle eye, also held fond memories of Lady Gladys during that spectacular season. She recalled her 'swooning' over Karsavina and Nijinsky, often lending the Coopers her box at the theatre so that she could get a closer view from the stalls.[19] Lady Gladys watched every performance of Nijinsky in *La Spectre de la Rose* that season.

And so it was that Lady Gladys and her daughter Juliet had every reason to celebrate as they watched from their regular box on that special Coronation Gala evening, and later that night among their society friends. Such friends included the Hon. Albert Henry Stopford, known to some as Bertie. A frequent guest at Lady Gladys's parties, and blessed with the right connections and similar tastes, he could always be relied upon to keep the others entertained with his infectious enthusiasm and kindly manner.

Stopford had known Lady Gladys and her husband Lord de Grey for many years and shared a number of influential friends at court. Lord de Grey was Treasurer to Queen Alexandra, while Stopford's father, Rector of the rural village of Titchmarsh in Northamptonshire, had been Chaplain Royal to Queen Victoria, Edward VII and now George V. His aunt, the Hon. Horatia Charlotte Stopford, was also known at court as maid of honour to Queen Victoria.

By 1911 Lord and Lady de Grey were well established in Coombe Court in an area on Coombe Hill not far from Twickenham, having moved from Bruton Street in 1901. The Coombe site had been developed by the father of the author John Galsworthy,[20] who built three large Victorian houses on the land. The de Greys were not the only residents of note in that affluent area. Next door, at Coombe Springs, lived Mrs Hwfa Williams. Her reputation in London's social circles was based not only on the lavish occasions that she organised all over the West End, but on the remarkably close relationship she had enjoyed with Edward VII – she was his favourite bridge partner – and his mistress Alice Keppel.

The third house, Coombe Warren, was an ornate building standing on a terrace at the top of Kingston Hill with a view stretching as far as the Epsom Downs. (Galsworthy himself had lived in one of the houses for some years and had based Robin Hill, Soames Forsyte's new house in *The Forsyte Saga*, on Coombe Warren.)

Not far away at Fulwell Park, the young King Manuel of Portugal made Twickenham his home in exile following a turbulent period in Lisbon. After his father and elder brother were assassinated, his own rule as monarch lasted only three years before he abdicated and fled to Gibraltar on his yacht. Manuel was another regular guest of the de Greys.

Charles Neilson Gattey, author of *Lady de Grey and the Garden's Golden Age*, captured the atmosphere of life at Coombe Court:

People came down there to have tea and stroll about and dine, and it seemed almost accidental that on the evening when the Princess of Wales came down to dine with [Lady Gladys], it happened to be an off night at the opera, and in consequence Melba and Jean de Reske were there too, and so after dinner there was a little singing. It was not so easy to hear either of them except at the opera, for Melba only took one private engagement a year when she sang at the house of Mr Alfred de Rothschild for a suitable sum, and Jean's appearance at a private concert was as rare. Those folk therefore who were privileged to hear them like this in mufti were very apt (and with good reason) to tell everyone how marvellously they had sung, and that was very good for the opera, while the divine choristers had been delighted to sing for the Princess of Wales.[21]

The influx of Russian nobility to London had also been a notable feature of the Edwardian period. Grand Duke Mikhail Mikhailovich, a distant relative of the Tsar, was already installed at Kenwood House near Hampstead; while in 1909 Prince Felix Felixovich Yusupov came to London before going up to Oxford University, with his cousin Prince Serge Obolensky following in his footsteps a few years later. Mrs Williams was quick to single out Prince Yusupov for attention the moment he arrived in London, and they were soon planning some very extravagant social occasions together.

Encouraged by Diaghilev's triumph at Covent Garden, Coombe Court continued to act as the hub of London's Anglo-Russian world. Bertie Stopford was spotted on occasion escorting Anna Pavlova and Tamara Karsavina around London, sometimes accompanying them to visit Lady Gladys at home. This was the beginning of his friendship with members of the *Ballets Russes*, including Diaghilev, an association that would continue under very different circumstances during and after the First World War.

Although in no way classically trained, Stopford had a fine reputation as a leader of cotillions at society balls. Encouraged by Mrs Hwfa Williams,[22] he was more than willing to demonstrate his skill at other dances too. One night, during the Diaghilev season, there was the usual crowd at Mrs Williams' house – Melba, Diaghilev, Karsavina, Manuel of Portugal, George of Greece, Lady Juliet Duff and Mrs John Jacob Astor among them. This was also the occasion of Serge Obolensky's first visit to the Williams' house, transported there from Covent Garden in luxurious style by Felix Yusupov in his smart new car, a Delone-Belleville.

Stopford had offered to escort Anna Pavlova to Mrs Williams' party after her performance that night. She was in 'a particularly gay mood' and, urged on by the guests, the prima ballerina performed 'a burlesque fandango' with the help of Stopford and Obolensky, who were happy to enter into the spirit of things:

> I could vaguely remember the steps from Maestro Ceccetti's teaching. I tied my coat tails round me and, with me on one side and Bertie on the other, Pavlova scored another theatrical triumph while we provided the comic relief.[23]

Later that evening Obolensky and Yusupov escorted Pavlova back to Felix's flat. Bertie Stopford, by this time, 'was nowhere to be seen'.[24] He was already going his own mysterious way after a party, a habit that was to have such terrible consequences for him in later life.

CHAPTER TWO

Titchmarsh

TWENTY-FIRST century networking, for business or social gain, has a deliberate, almost creative edge to it. Contacts are built up using a combination of determination, planning and energy. Not so the Victorian and Edwardian society network, with its reliance on family connections. Such connections would be considered essential to one's standing in society and could certainly be worked to great advantage, as Albert Stopford discovered.

The second son of the newly appointed curate of St John's church in Peterborough, Albert Henry Stopford was born into a well-to-do, though not excessively wealthy, family. They did, however, have connections. Within a year of Albert's birth on 16 May 1860, his father had been presented with a living as Rector of Titchmarsh in nearby Northamptonshire by Lord Lilford. A year later he was appointed Chaplain Royal to Queen Victoria, a position he held until he died, serving Edward VII and George V during that time.

The Stopfords were perhaps no ordinary family. Stopford was the family name of the Earls of Courtown, an Irish peerage, and Albert's father, Reverend Frederick Manners Stopford,[1] was himself a cousin of the 5th Earl of Courtown. The family can claim common ancestry with the late Queen Mother, Elizabeth Bowes Lyon, with a line that is possible to trace all the way back to Charles II. Albert's grandfather was a colonel in the Scots Guards who had fought at Waterloo, a regimental connection Albert was very proud of. His aunt, Horatia Charlotte Stopford, had been responsible, as maid of honour to Queen Victoria, for recommending her brother Frederick to her contacts at Windsor; while their uncle, Richard Bruce Stopford, set a family precedent many years before Frederick, as a chaplain to the Queen. In an age of primogeniture such connections were an essential substitute for landed wealth which inevitably went to the eldest son.

Titchmarsh, where Albert was brought up, remains a delightful English village, with its rows of cottages, some thatched, which are built of an attractive mellow stone. The cottages are overlooked by the imposing church of St Mary The Virgin,[2] dating back to the days of the Normans, and a newly rebuilt rectory within its own spacious grounds, farming land and stables. The poet John Dryden is recorded as having lived in the village in the seventeenth century.

In Stopford's day, however, Titchmarsh was still feudal, with a lord of the manor, rector and a few farming families, labourers and artisans – some 900 souls in all.[3] By the mid-nineteenth century the lord of the manor, or recipient of rents or tithes, Lord Lilford, was no longer resident in the village but lived nearby. His son Thomas Powys had been a close friend of Frederick Stopford when they were up at Christ Church, Oxford together in the late 1850s. When Thomas succeeded his father to the title in 1861, he appointed his college friend to the rectory within the same year.

A rector's way of life was comfortable without being extravagant and, by all accounts, Frederick brought to it a keen sense of duty combined with the enthusiasm of a young priest. To crown the appointment he was given permission during his first year in Titchmarsh to knock down the old Jacobean-style rectory, riddled with woodworm and dry rot, and replace it with a new building.

What Frederick Stopford built can best be described as Victorian Gothic, with ample room for a large family. He could even afford a housemaid, cook and kitchen maid, a domestic nurse and governess for the children, as well as a live-in coachman and gardener. The rector's study, in a prime position on the ground floor, overlooked a well-kept lawn featuring a spectacular cedar tree over two hundred years old, with branches spreading outwards over seventy feet. Locals boasted that the outer circumference of the branches was

TITCHMARSH

The rectory and family home at Titchmarsh, built under the supervision of the Rev. Frederick Stopford, Albert's father.

(© W. Clarke)

close to a hundred yards. It was just the kind of view to inspire a newly appointed chaplain to the monarch as he prepared his annual sermon for the Chapel Royal in St James's Palace.

The new rectory was soon echoing to the shouts and laughter of a growing family. Albert Stopford was the second child of nine, and he and elder brother Algernon Edward were born in London before their parents moved to Titchmarsh. The next brother Francis arrived in 1861 as the rebuilding was nearing completion. His other siblings were all born at the rectory.[4]

One of Albert's earliest childhood memories of the rectory was the ringing of the church bells to greet the return of his mother and new baby brother Francis from London.[5] The bells were an important feature of rural life. Apart from the regular Sunday peals, they announced the death of villagers, even spelling out the age and sex of the departed. Albert's mother often arranged suppers for the bell-ringers, who were held in high esteem.

Titchmarsh was a traditional village, especially on religious occasions. The autumn harvest festival took the form of a procession that began in front of the rectory, winding its way slowly around the village before entering the church for the service.[6]

The Stopford children were encouraged to take part in village life whenever occasion demanded it, following the example of their mother who organised Sunday school lessons for the local children. In their first year at the rectory, as the rebuilding of the house was underway and the gardens were being relaid, the Stopfords invited villagers to visit after church on Sunday to observe the latest improvements. This invitation soon became a tradition, and one that was still observed until relatively recently.[7]

As Albert grew up and the family increased in size, he maintained a natural affinity with his elder brother Algernon, two years older, and Francis, one year younger. In such a rambling house the brothers could find mystery and adventure around every corner, and the flooded rectory cellars were a favourite haunt. Francis later recalled that 'one of the greatest adventures of my childhood, after a thaw or heavy rain, was tying boxes to my boots, to wade through the waters in the darkness of the beer cellar. I fancied I was exploring the murky caverns of the sea.'[8]

Although a source of delight to the boys, the water in the cellars was to prove a very serious hazard for the rector and his wife when the household was struck down with acute sewage poisoning. By good fortune the water was quickly analysed and the mischief discovered. The builder of the original house had constructed the main sewage pipes over the wells outside the back door, the source of the household's water supply, to a cesspit under the elms by the cow-yard gate. 'Why none of us children died,' Francis later wrote, 'goodness knows; probably it was the wonderful life-giving power of Titchmarsh air, a fact you quickly realise when you wander about the churchyard and read the ages on the headstones.'[9]

The seven brothers had a short spell with a tutor before leaving the family home at an early age to succumb to the rigours of a private school.[10] Having been a foundation scholar at Charterhouse himself, their father believed that a similar education would suit his sons, whether at Charterhouse, nearby Oundle, or elsewhere.

The girls Eveleen and Mary, on the other hand, were left in the hands of a governess. Remaining closer to home they took part more regularly in local events than the boys. Such occasions varied from dances in the village hall (the 'Clubroom'), to concerts and what were known as 'penny readings'. The church choir was also a feature of village life, sometimes singing from the top of the church tower; and plays were often performed, organised by the Stopford sisters.

Despite school commitments Albert participated as often as he could in the social calendar of an active church and village, while at the same time developing his contacts with members of the extended family such as the Stopford-Sackvilles at Dreyton House, the Powys family at Lilford Hall, and the Watsons at Rockingham Castle. There were also the relatives of his mother, the Saunders family, at Westbourne Lodge in the south. Albert's mother Florence sadly died when he was just sixteen, and his father was to marry Caroline, a Saunders cousin, a couple of years later.

Albert appeared to be very aware of the value of family networks when it came to meeting 'the right sort of people'. With instinctive social skills and a determination to live life to the full, he set out to establish a career for himself, taking every possible opportunity to cultivate acquaintances who might extend his social horizons.

It was also during these formative years that he began to recognise his homosexuality. In order to develop an agreeable career and to conduct his social life with discretion, he knew that he would have to move to the relative anonymity of a large metropolis. For Albert, London was the obvious choice, the city where his father and aunt had already established their own social and royal networks.

By 1894, however, Stopford was in his mid-thirties and had left London for Paris, already established in business as a dealer in antiques. Using the French capital as a base, and with a useful fluency in the language, he travelled extensively throughout Europe for business and pleasure. With occasional trips to London, and winter breaks on the island of Sicily and French Riviera, Albert Stopford was looked upon by many as both highly cultured and upwardly mobile.

CARTIER IN THE RUE DE LA PAIX

Known as one of the finest streets in Paris, the rue
de la Paix is viewed here from the Place de l'Opera.
Cartier, the maker of exquisite jewellery for the rich
and famous, moved its business to this area in 1899.

(© Popperfoto/Getty Images)

CHAPTER THREE

Fabergé and Cartier

THERE is a tantalising gap in the life of Albert Stopford during his twenties. He is fleetingly recorded as lodging with a retired farmer's wife in the Paddington district of London at the age of twenty. He is also noted in the 1881 Census as being employed locally as a mercantile clerk. Ten years later, however, in the Census of 1891, Albert Stopford is listed as staying at the Metropole Hotel in Brighton with a valet, and as being of 'independent means'.[1]

The positions held by Stopford's father and aunt at court had continued to increase the family's stock, and Albert's presence was noted occasionally at society weddings and memorial services, sometimes linked to the Guards regiments or with a member of the Royal family. On 26 June 1886, 'The Court Circular' in *The Times* reported that Albert Stopford had recently attended a levee at St James's Palace, where he had been presented to Edward, Prince of Wales by Lord Howard of Glossop. The Circular was at pains to point out that this was the same as being presented to the Queen.[2]

By the time Stopford reached thirty in 1890, he appeared to be well established in the West End of London as a dealer in antique furniture and *objets d'art*, and growing in status and affluence. His business was located just around the corner from Bruton Street where Lady Gladys lived (initially as the Countess of Lonsdale, and then from 1885 as Lady de Grey).

By 1894, however, Stopford was more or less living in Paris. What prompted him to leave London for the French capital might simply have been the demands of his antiques business. However, it is much more likely to have been the result of a sexual indiscretion in the same year. A warrant had been issued for his arrest after he was accused of a homosexual act with a young Scots Guardsman in Windsor.[3] The warrant, however, was not carried out. The fact that it was withdrawn three years later strongly suggests that Stopford had gone abroad to let matters cool down. Whatever the reason for his departure, he could not have been well enough known to attract the attention of the gossip columns, and it plainly had no lasting effect on his social standing at the time.

In October of 1901 Stopford was once again listed in *The Times* among the guests at a society event, this time at the wedding of Helen Morton, daughter of a former Vice President of the United States, and the Comte Boson de Perigord.[4] For a mercantile clerk turned antiques dealer, his presence on their guest list was impressive. Was it all down to family connections?

It has already been noted that his dancing prowess had caught the eye of the likes of Mrs Hwfa Williams. Her lavish parties, both at home in Coombe Springs and in the West End of London, provided ample opportunity for Stopford to demonstrate his talents in the cotillion or French quadrille. As his reputation spread, other fashionable cities beckoned. On a visit to New York in 1905 Stopford's presence was welcomed by leading society hosts including James H. Hyde, who invited the Englishman to a lavish French eighteenth-century ball at fashionable Sherry's restaurant on West 44th Street. Lady guests were encouraged to affect a Versailles look by dressing in court gowns complete with powdered hair, while the men wore court or hunt costumes.[5] According to the *New York Times*, Stopford's next engagement was at a small dinner party given for Viscountess Maitland by Mrs Henry Siegel, this time inspired by the theme of a Japanese garden. Among the thirty or so guests, Albert Henry Stopford was described as the cotillion leader from London.[6]

Stopford's reputation as a dancer continued right up to 1913 when his presence was noted at a dinner ball at the Ritz in Paris given by a Mrs Alistair Paget (formerly Whitney) and her sister-in-law Lady Colebrook. Among the guests were two sons of the Russian Grand Duchess Maria Pavlovna – Kyril and Boris Vladimirovich – as well as Grand Duke Dmitri Pavlovich (cousin of Tsar Nicholas), the Duchess of Marlborough, and Mrs William B. Leeds (soon to become Princess Anastasia of Greece). The *New York Times* reported once again that Stopford led a cotillion at the end of the ball.[7]

Stopford was already acquainted with Grand Duchess Maria Pavlovna. It is possible that they first met in Paris, where Maria often stayed. Stopford, Maria Pavlovna and Lady Gladys de Grey shared a passion for jewellery, opera and ballet, and Stopford's dealings in French and Russian *objets d'art* probably contributed to their mutual friendship.

Lady Gladys and her husband were enthusiastic collectors of the St Petersburg jeweller Fabergé's unique works of art, an enthusiasm shared by Queen Alexandra. They were all regular visitors to the company's premises in London – in Duke Street, then Dover Street, and finally New Bond Street. Albert Stopford was also a frequent customer, buying Fabergé's latest creations for himself, and on behalf of his affluent clients.

The fascination in the work of Peter Karl Fabergé and his Russian craftsmen in St Petersburg[8] has been established by the fame of the fifty-seven fabulous Easter eggs commissioned for the families of Tsar Alexander III and his son Nicholas II, and the subsequent fate of the eggs. Although nearly half of the original pieces are now back in Russia, thanks to the buying power of one of the newly established Russian tycoons, for a long time there were less than a dozen in Russian hands.

The Fabergé business was founded in St Petersburg in 1842 by Gustav Fabergé (1814-93), who came from a refugee Huguenot family. At the end of the nineteenth century, however, his son Karl had expanded the company, bringing in some of the finest jewellery makers in the Russian capital, such as Yuli Rappoport, Heinrik Wigström, Erik Kolin, August Holmström and Mikhail E. Perkhin. Karl Fabergé was renowned for the way he transformed the craft of jeweller and goldsmith into unique pieces that distinguished his work from all other rivals. Described as works of fantasy, each piece owed more to its artistic character than to the value of the stones and materials used in its production. The work ranged from the intricate and world-famous Easter eggs, to flowers, animals and birds, children, music boxes, brooches, picture frames, clocks and cigarette lighters – some fashioned out of hardstone, others with refined enamelling on a metallic base of silver or gold. On one visit to Dover Street, Stopford acquired a penguin, duckling, owl, pig, cornflower and a bear, all fashioned in Fabergé's inimitable style.[9]

When Tsar Alexander bought the first of the specially crafted 'surprise' Easter eggs from Fabergé in the mid-1880s as a present for his wife Maria Feodorovna, others at court quickly followed his lead, invariably finding some unusual or special gift in the Fabergé emporium. It thus came as no surprise when Fabergé was appointed Supplier to the Court of His Imperial Highness in 1885.

What was deemed fashionable at the Russian court soon became popular elsewhere in Europe. The merest glance through the names of clients in Fabergé's well-preserved London account books[10] reveals a who's who of Victorian and Edwardian aristocracy and other far-flung monarchs. A colourful description of Fabergé's establishment on the first floor of the building in Dover Street was written by the joint manager at the time:

> In those Edwardian days Kings and Queens and Royal princes ... walked upstairs and knocked on the door with their knuckles.
> It used to be exciting. Was it the postman or the Shah of Persia? It became so exciting and appeared to be so in keeping with my royal visitors' expectations that I never made any alteration in our procedure. So everyone kept knocking at the door. ... It was here, quite unknown to the passing crowd in Piccadilly, that Kings put aside their crowns, that ambassadors, maharajahs and magnates of all

kinds, gay lords, grave lords, law-lords, and the lords of the Daily Press, cast off their chains of office and spent a cool and refreshing half hour. … I remember one late afternoon in particular when [Queen Alexandra] brought with her the King and Queen of Norway, the King of Greece, the King of Denmark and, if I remember rightly, Princess Victoria and Miss Charlotte Knollys. It is always the little things which stick in one's memory. 'May we open the drawers?' the Queen asked.[11]

Other visitors included the King of Portugal and the Queen of Italy. Edward VII was also a regular customer when searching for something special for Queen Alexandra for a birthday, anniversary or event. Occasionally the couple would commission a unique piece, such as a Fabergé rendition of Edward's shooting pony Iron Duke made in orletz on a nephrite base. They even requested a model of a Chelsea Pensioner. During one visit in 1909 the Queen spent £35,000 (almost £2 million today). Society friends like the de Greys also added to the Royal collection with the occasional gift, and by the time of her death in 1925 Queen Alexandra had accumulated one of the largest collections of Fabergé in Europe.

Regular visitors to Fabergé in London also included Leopold de Rothschild, Sir Ernest Cassel, Lord Revelstoke, the Duke of Norfolk, Lord Iveagh, Lady Sackville, Mrs Hwfa Williams, Mrs George Keppel, Lady Juliet Duff and London-based Grand Duke Mikhail Mikhailovich. It also attracted other members of the Russian court on their fleeting visits to Britain, including Nicholas II's mother Empress Maria Feodorovna, as well as Stopford's particular acquaintance the Grand Duchess Maria Pavlovna and her sons Kyril and Boris Vladimirovich.[12]

Maria Pavlovna was already a devotee of Fabergé and had been a growing admirer of the work of Louis-François Cartier, the leading French jeweller based in Paris, since her first visit in 1900. The French capital had become an increasing attraction for Russian nobility in the latter decades of the nineteenth century, keen to purchase the latest fashions. Whether wintering on the French Riviera or visiting European spas, they would often include a visit to the Cartier establishment as part of their itinerary.

The Parisian jeweller's first Russian customer was recorded as early as 1860 when a Prince Soltikov called in to purchase an emerald bracelet with a black enamelled gold setting. From then, Cartier's reputation spread to the Russian Imperial court, where eagerly awaited deliveries from Paris would soon become part of the traditional Christmas festivities.

Louis-François Cartier's son Alfred took over the business in 1874 and by the end of the 1890s it was sufficiently well-established to contemplate a move from the boulevard des Italiens to larger premises in the rue de la Paix.[13] This was already one of the most fashionable streets in Paris, and home to leading jewellers, fashion houses, shoemakers and perfume manufacturers, all surrounded by high class hotels. It would soon be enhanced by the grand opening of the Paris Ritz Hotel in the Place Vendome in 1898.

By this time Alfred's eldest son Louis had joined the business. Such dignitaries as the future King Edward VII and Grand Duchess Maria Pavlovna enjoyed a personal greeting from Louis in his private office beyond the entrance hall. On one occasion, according to Louis,

> … the Grand Duke [Pavel Alexandrovich] and his wife, the Countess of Hohenfelsen [Olga Valerianovna Pistolkors], were sitting in my office, having ordered a magnificent sapphire tiara for [Pavel's] daughter. … To my amazement, the Grand Duke, who was sitting close to the half-open door, suddenly called out the name 'Arthur' to somebody. A dignified-looking Englishman turned round in surprise at hearing his name called. It was the Duke of Connaught, brother of Edward VII. The two princes shook hands delighted at the unexpected meeting.[14]

One of Maria Pavlovna's early purchases at Cartier was a Russian double-eagle pearl necklace which was shown privately to a few friends and customers of the company before being despatched to St Petersburg. On her trips to Paris, Maria often graced receptions at the Russian Embassy where, among orchids specially shipped over from the Crimea, she was pleased to show off her latest Cartier purchase.

In 1903 the Russian Grand Duke Alexei Mikhailovich was recorded as having bought a serpent monocle, and in 1906 the Grand Duchess Xenia Alexandrovna (sister of Tsar Nicholas) paid her first visit to Cartier. She was followed the next year by her mother, Empress Maria Feodorovna, while staying in the Villa Espoir in Biarritz. Such visits prompted Cartier's Russian clients to wonder why the French jeweller did not open a permanent branch in St Petersburg, a thought pressed on the firm by Grand Duchess Maria Pavlovna in particular. The idea had in fact already occurred to Louis Cartier, following a number of personal visits to the Russian capital during the Christmas period and spring season. The success of a special Cartier exhibition at the Grand Hôtel de l'Europe in 1907, and the consequent acquisition of the Tsar's warrant, convinced him to take the idea forward.

Grand Duchess Maria Pavlovna's custom continued to grow. She had already introduced Cartier to her family, and the company had supplied her personally with a briolette aigrette tiara, a tiara made of rubies, and a sapphire *kokoshnik* or Russian-style tiara. In 1908 she provided Cartier with rented premises in one of her own buildings on the Quai de la Cour in St Petersburg. Not long after that, on the recommendation of Empress Maria Feodorovna, who was a recent devotee, Cartier's representative in the Russian capital was granted an audience with Tsar Nicholas and his wife Alexandra.

When Louis Cartier visited St Petersburg the following year, Maria Pavlovna arranged for him to take part in her annual Christmas charity sale, at which the cream of Russian society would be present. Cartier was deeply impressed. One of the visitors was the Duchess of Leuchtenberg. 'Guess whose necklace she's wearing,' Maria Pavlovna whispered to Cartier. The Parisian jeweller confessed he had no idea. 'It was, would you believe it, the one which Napoleon had given the Empress Josephine'. He noted too the bewildering number of Russian aristocrats who presented themselves to him that evening:

> [I] sat down at the table with Princess Demidova and Princess [Belosselsky], where we received a visit from the Empress Maria Feodorovna, Grand Duke Mikhail Mikhailovich and many other Grand Dukes whom I never saw in Paris.[15]

Cartier's growing success in St Petersburg increased demand for stones, enamel and gold work from Russia for their French premises. Even Fabergé was asked to supply materials. Although regarded as a competitor, the latter concentrated more on *objets d'art* than jewellery and was more than happy to fulfil Cartier orders.

Albert Stopford followed these developments with great interest from his base in Paris. His contacts in the art world, and in Russian society circles in the French capital, had already alerted him to the potential for furthering his antique-dealing activities both in London, Paris, and now St Petersburg. His acquaintance with Maria Pavlovna would also create wider commercial opportunities for him as Cartier extended their custom eastward and Russian taste and influence began to take hold in the West. Cartier could no longer ignore Fabergé's more specialised market, and the French company appeared keen to develop some of Fabergé's techniques.

It was not long before Albert Stopford was added to the list of suppliers of Fabergé products to Cartier, leaning on his Russian connections and Parisian residence to support his case. His name can be found in a number of Cartier's records for the years leading up to the First World War.[16]

In the interest of business Stopford first visited St Petersburg in 1909, and was recorded there once again in the early months of 1914. Although work doubtless came first, he regarded socialising in the capital as an essential part of his trip. In November 1913, in preparation for a second visit, Stopford treated fourteen guests to an extravagant lunch at the Savoy in London.[17] His invitees included

Maria Pavlovna, her son Boris, the President of Serbia, Prince Serge Obolensky, Lady Juliet Duff, Lady Muriel Paget and Mrs Nancy B. Leeds. It was a chance to renew acquaintances in London, but there was perhaps more to his extravagant gesture. As it turned out, many of those present at the Savoy were set to play significant roles in Stopford's life in the very near future.

The diners remembered their host that day with a mixture of admiration and affection. He was just Bertie, the dancer, the extrovert, the confirmed bachelor, someone who moved in their circles.

At the same time, Stopford's father, the Reverend Frederick, was likewise remembering his son in terms of his social standing. When he came to draw up his last will and testament in Titchmarsh, he left Albert out of his bequests on the grounds that he already 'had sufficient funds for all his needs'.[18] One can perhaps understand his father's reasoning. From the distance of sleepy Titchmarsh, Albert Stopford's opulent lifestyle must have raised many an eyebrow.

'THE RACE OF THE TURKISH REFUGEES'

A train besieged by Turkish soldiers retreating from
Lule Burgas at the Front to the relative safety of
Constantinople.

(*Illustrated London News*, 9 November 1912)

CHAPTER FOUR

Balkan Intelligence

ALBERT Stopford's social and business networks in London, Paris and St Petersburg before the First World War were anchored in his friendship with Lady Gladys and Grand Duchess Maria Pavlovna. But they were not his only means of establishing useful contacts, as his business activities abroad gave him access to information that might be of use to the intelligence community.

Stopford was employed in his early career as a mercantile clerk dealing with shipping insurance. This most probably brought him into contact with members of Lloyds Maritime Intelligence Services (LMIS), a worldwide network of agents and sources who supplied information on naval and maritime matters to Lloyd's head office in London. From this it is possible to infer that Stopford could have moved from his position as clerk to becoming a regular informant for Lloyds through LMIS.

Although primarily a commercial organisation, the eyes and ears of the well-known London insurance market, LMIS worked closely with the British Admiralty's intelligence departments and had concluded an agreement with the Admiralty in 1901 to share information gathered on a regular basis. This hints at an increasingly shadowy interest in foreign military affairs for Stopford, culminating in a visit he made to the Balkan states in 1912. Correspondence sent to Maria Pavlovna by Stopford from the area, currently held in the Russian State Archives, forms the basis of what is known about his whereabouts and actions during this politically charged time.[1] It strongly suggests that Albert Stopford and Maria Pavlovna had far more in common than *objets d'art* and ballet.

Politics had always been a subject close to Maria's heart. She was born Marie Alexandrine Elisabeth Eleonore of the German House of Mecklenburg-Schwerin in 1854 to Grand Duke Friedrich Franz II and Princess Augusta of Ruess-Köstritz. Her marriage in 1874 to Grand Duke Vladimir Alexandrovich of Russia brought her to a position of political influence within the Imperial family as the wife of Tsar Alexander III's brother, and she took the Russian name Maria Pavlovna in recognition of her adopted country. With the accession of Nicholas II to the throne in 1894, Vladimir and Maria were uncle and aunt ('Aunt Miechen') to the young Tsar, a highly educated, charming young man, but a fatalist who was flawed by indecision. When Alexander III died unexpectedly at forty-nine, his son was ill-prepared to take the throne. Alexander, having ruthlessly revoked his own father's liberal reforms, had left the country politically stable with a growing economy. But lacking faith in his own ability, Nicholas resolved to rule as his father had – as an autocrat – although he had little of Alexander's strength of character.

This gave Nicholas's uncles and other elder statesmen more influence in the running of the country, and Vladimir and Maria willingly embraced the world of politics and culture. Vladimir, a former military leader, was also a respected painter, collector of ikons, and patron of the ballet. His long-held appointment as President of the Imperial Academy of Art enabled the couple to provide direct support to the Imperial Russian Ballet, and later to Sergei Diaghilev for the *Ballets Russes*. This continued until Vladimir died in 1909.

Both Maria and Vladimir appeared as comfortable at home in St Petersburg as in the boulevards of Paris, where they usually stayed at the Continental Hotel on rue Castiglione. Travelling in their own coach attached to the Express du Nord between St Petersburg, Berlin and Paris, they met with statesmen and cultural figures at a succession of glittering occasions in European capitals.

For Maria Pavlovna the world of politics and royal accession was as much a passion as the arts. She was pragmatic in her approach, particularly in relation to her sons and their path to the throne, and prepared to alter her stance if beneficial to her family. It was said, for example, that she refused to give up Lutheranism in favour of Russian Orthodoxy on her marriage to Vladimir. But when Kyril miraculously survived a shipwreck during the 1904-05 Russo-Japanese war, Maria claimed the power of Orthodox prayer had saved her son and she converted. Her action, however, may have had more to do with her desire to have Kyril reinstated to the line of succession after he married his cousin, the divorcee Victoria Melita, and incurred the anger of the Tsar.

From 1912-14 Maria took a particular interest in political events within the Balkan territories, as members of her own family would be directly affected by a war in the region. Maria's daughter Elena (Helen) Vladimirovna had been married to Prince Nicholas of Greece since 1902, while Vladimir's niece Maria, daughter of Maria Alexandrovna, was married to the future King Ferdinand I of Romania. Stopford also recalled Maria Pavlovna showing great interest in a royal match between Princess Eleonore Ruess-Köstritz of Saxe-Coburg-Gotha and Ferdinand I of Bulgaria.

The so-called 'Eastern' or 'Balkan Question' was also a matter of political concern for the 'Great Powers' (Britain, Russia, Austria-Hungary, Germany, France and Italy), who all had vastly different aspirations for the area.

In the past, Britain had attempted a mediatory role in the many crises that occurred in the Balkans, in a bid to maintain the *status quo*. Having strong trade links with the Ottoman Empire, Britain was resistant to change and did not wish to see another country controlling the straits of the Dardanelles. Russia, however, wanted exclusive access to warm-water ports via the Dardanelles to safeguard trade and military interests, and stood to benefit from the collapse of the Empire. The two countries were nonetheless united in their desire to protect Christians in the Empire from persecution.

In the spring of 1912 the Christian Balkan states of Bulgaria and Serbia signed treaties of mutual assistance to seize Albania, Macedonia and Thrace from the Ottoman Empire. Russia, although initially supportive, withdrew its support in protest against the perceived threat of a stronger and united Balkans when Greece and Macedonia also signed up.

The countries in the so-called Balkan League were also motivated by territorial gain and were greatly encouraged by the recent defeat of Turkey during the Italo-Turkish War (1911-12). The Ottoman Empire was also weakened by ongoing political instability, and a call for constitutional rule and more effective modernisation by a group of liberals and reformers known as the Young Turks had forced Sultan Adbul Hamid II to abdicate in 1909.

Due to the lack of a coherent plan or co-ordination of effort, it was Montenegro alone who declared war on Turkey on 8 October. The remaining Balkan allies joined the conflict on 17 October.

Given his work as a mercantile clerk and links with LMIS, Stopford would have known how important the Balkans and its access routes were to Britain and other countries. But he was also aware of Maria Pavlovna's interest. As soon as Montenegro declared war Stopford wrote to her from Paris about his intention to go to the area, adding that the Paris Bourse had suffered its biggest fall in almost a quarter of a century as a result of the war.[2]

Stopford sailed to Constantinople via Corfu and then Athens. On the outward journey, he sent a number of postcards to Maria and a message to Helen, alerting her to his visit. Although not in the city, a note was left with her chamberlain thanking Stopford for all that he was doing for her mother. She had gone to Salonika to be with her in-laws, George of the Hellenes and Olga Konstantinova, to celebrate the capture of the former Turkish-controlled city by the Greek Army.[3]

Stopford left boxes of chocolates for Helen, and booked himself into the Grand Bretagne Hotel on Syngatma Square. From there he

wrote Maria a lengthy letter, describing the successes of the Greek troops and the scenes of jubilation on the streets of Athens. But success, he said, had come at a cost, for there had been many casualties. From what he had witnessed, the hospitals were full to overflowing and the Red Cross was struggling to cope.[4]

Moving on to Constantinople, Stopford saw the Great Powers' 'men o' war' anchored in the Dardanelles, sent into the area ostensibly to protect foreign nationals. Although there was some truth in this claim, each country had political reasons for their presence.

Stopford had little trouble getting accommodation at the French-run Pera Palace Hotel, from where he could see the magnificent Santa Sophia mosque, a possible target for the encroaching Bulgarian Army. He looked for a war correspondent to get the latest news from the Front, although this proved difficult as most of the foreign press corps had been cut off by the fighting. The correspondent from the *Morning Post* was around, however, and agreed to brief him on any developments. Stopford advised Maria to read the *Post* for the latest news.[5]

The weakness of the Ottoman Empire, which had partly attracted the Montenegrin attack in the first place, was soon demonstrated on the battlefield as the Turkish Army began to suffer heavy losses. Constantinople itself, reeling from the news of continuous defeats, appeared strangely calm. Stopford's hotel was barely half-full and people were going about their business largely unconcerned.[6] Stopford was beginning to think that the recent landing of troops from the allied fleets in the Dardanelles was perhaps unnecessary.

But when Stopford hired the services of a local guide to drive down to Santa Sophia, he found the area to be in such stark contrast to the rest of the city and crowded with refugees and wounded soldiers. One group of men, their feet raw and bleeding, sat in abject silence. The makeshift camp was rife with cholera and dysentery.

Stopford persuaded the *Morning Post* correspondent to take him up to the front line, possibly to Lule Burgas (29-31 October), a horrifying experience after the relative calm of Constantinople. The explosion of shells and incessant thunder of gunfire over the battlefield made survival difficult to imagine amid such carnage. The authorities were utterly overwhelmed.[7] Stopford could see evidence all around him of woeful neglect, with soldiers lying for days in the mud, succumbing to festering wounds or cholera. More than three hundred dead and dying men were dealt with by being thrown out of a train and rolled down an embankment.[8]

Stopford described the scene in a letter to Maria. It was, he said, like the terrible destruction of Messina during the 1908 earthquake.[9] And as a regular visitor to Sicily, he may well have been there at the time of the disaster, or witnessed its devastating aftermath.

Stopford was able to let Maria[10] know that bread and charcoal was being distributed to the families of Turkish soldiers from a fund organised by Lady Alice Lowther, wife of the British Ambassador in Constantinople. Stopford had taken sugar plums for the children and was slightly embarrassed by their gratitude. But what upset him most was the appalling lack of information given to the families of the Turkish soldiers, who only found out that loved ones were injured, even killed, by hearsay or rumour.

Lady Lowther's fund was involved in making arrangements for refugee families to be sent to Anatolia. Stopford considered staying on to help with the evacuation, but he could not speak Turkish. With the feeling that he could do little more to help, he returned to Paris.

By 18 November the Bulgarian Army had advanced to within ten miles of Constantinople. In response, the British Naval Brigade landed at Constantinople and took up quarters in the grounds of the British Embassy. The other Great Powers followed, and a joint plan was drawn up to protect the city. The Balkan League had made territorial gains, but it was clear that they would not be permitted to take Constantinople and hostilities were suspended. An armistice was agreed between the Ottoman Empire and Balkan League at the beginning of December, leading to a peace conference in London.

The Young Turks' *coup d'etat* in Constantinople the following January led to a resumption of hostilities, but in the wake of further defeats, Turkey agreed to sign a Peace Treaty in London in May 1913. As a result the Ottoman Empire lost virtually all of its European territory.

Stopford's final letter to Maria Pavlovna from Constantinople was sent five days before the first armistice, asking if they might meet up on his return to Paris. His Balkan trip had marked a change in the nature of their relationship, and he could now be regarded as a trustworthy source of information. Whether Maria thought she was the only person to benefit from his trip, we shall never know, but it hardly seems credible that her needs alone would have prompted Stopford to suspend his business commitments to travel out to a war zone as soon the first shot was fired.

His reasons were more than likely connected to his earlier dealings with Lloyds Maritime Intelligence Services. It is well documented that maritime-based intelligence was at work during the years leading up to the First World War, and if it is assumed that Stopford had earlier dealings with LMIS, his Balkan venture may well have been a reconnaissance trip on behalf of intelligence operations.

Eighteen months later, Stopford would be involved once again in the shadowy world of intelligence – this time during the catastrophic 'war to end all wars'.

**PRINCE FELIX YUSUPOV
AND PRINCESS IRINA YUSUPOV**

Felix Yusupov and Irina Alexandrovna were married
on 22 February 1914. Their only child, Irina Felixovna
Yusupova (Bébé), was born on 21 March 1915 in
Petrograd.

(Library of Congress)

CHAPTER FIVE

Yusupov and Obolensky

I T was through the Anglo-Russian network in London that Albert Stopford first met the impressively titled Prince Felix Felixovich (Sumarokov-Elston) Yusupov and his more demure cousin Prince Serge Platonovich Obolensky.

Felix Yusupov was the younger son of Russia's richest family, and as such the pressure of responsibility did not sit heavily on his shoulders. All this was set to change, however, when in 1908 the 21-year-old prince experienced a terrible family tragedy.

That year, partly through the impulsive, some would say irresponsible, meddling of Felix, his older brother Nicolas had become emotionally involved with the Countess Marina de Heyden, whose forthcoming marriage to Count Arvid Mantueffel of the Horse Guards had already been announced. Stirring the romantic pot even more vigorously, Felix arranged for Marina to meet himself and Nicolas on the night before her wedding for a clandestine dinner in a private room of a fashionable restaurant.[1]

After the wedding was celebrated and the first days of her honeymoon in Paris had passed, Marina became increasingly troubled that she had married the wrong man. Frantic cables were sent to Nicolas and to her mother, pleading with them to come quickly to Paris. When Marina and Nicolas were spotted out together in the French capital, the consequences of their involvement began to unfold. In spite of family attempts to reconcile all egos involved, the scandal made the columns of the French and Russian newspapers. As rumours began to circulate around St Petersburg society, any attempt to hush the matter was surely now in vain.

As an officer of the Guards, Mantueffel felt obliged to defend his honour. The gauntlet was thrown down and the two men arranged to fight a duel at dawn on 22 June [Old Style calendar]* on Krestovsky Island, part of Prince Belosselsky-Belozersky's estate not far from St Petersburg. The weapon of choice was a revolver.

Just before eight in the morning the two men met at the chosen spot, accompanied by their seconds. Walking fifteen paces in opposite directions, they turned to fire. Nicolas deliberately shot into the

*NOTE ON DATES

For an explanation of the usage of the Old Style/New Style calendar within this publication, see page 44.

air. Count Mantueffel fired but missed. At the second attempt Nicolas again fired into the air, but Mantueffel took better aim this time and shot Nicolas through the heart. Felix had, in a split second, succeeded his elder brother as heir to the family's vast fortune.

Felix's tragic, even culpable, role in his brother's death eventually drove him to leave St Petersburg to make something of his life. Oxford University had been recommended by a close friend and so he decided to embrace the academic world. After stopping briefly in Paris along the way, Felix spent a month in London making the necessary arrangements to go up to university. He took rooms at the Carlton Hotel, then a new luxury establishment at the bottom of the Haymarket, vying with the Ritz and the Savoy.

While in London, Yusupov was grateful for the support of Arthur Winningham-Ingram, Bishop of London, who eased the young man's way in and around Oxford and introduced him to University College. The Bishop also brought Felix to the attention of a young Englishman, Eric Hamilton, later Dean of Windsor and Bishop of Salisbury, who was to become one of Yusupov's closest friends at the college.

Felix settled in Oxford in 1909 and was allotted a comfortable room with mullioned windows on the ground floor directly overlooking the main street, 'The High', with a smaller room attached. The Master of the College, who felt obliged to remain on hand to look after such an unusual student, told him that the larger room was known as the 'Club'. Regardless of occupant, the other students would meet there regularly to drink whisky.[2]

Yusupov needed little encouragement to keep up tradition. He arranged the small room into his bedroom, and kept the larger room as a living-room. He hired a piano, bought a few flowers and 'managed to make my rather cold and impersonal quarters look quite cosy and pleasant. That same evening the "Club" was filled with undergraduates who sang, drank and chattered until dawn.'[3] Sometimes Yusupov entertained them extravagantly; at other times he would take out his guitar and sing gypsy songs, 'with a quiet directness, like a Russian Bing Crosby'.[4]

Yusupov's irrepressibly high spirits led to many a late night carousing outwith the college and the consequent problem of getting back undetected. With three late nights leading to expulsion, Yusupov quickly notched up two. Then coming back to college hours after curfew from yet another dinner in London, Yusupov and a friend crashed into the closed gates of a level crossing in the fog. Felix was knocked unconscious, while his friend ended up in Oxford Hospital with several broken limbs. The car was a write-off.

In view of the near tragedy, Yusupov was excused his lateness this time, but after the next misdemeanour the Bishop of London was required to intervene to prevent his expulsion.

Yusupov maintained the 'Club' for his first year before, as customary, moving into outside accommodation for his second and third. Studying English and Forestry, then English alone, reports suggest that he fitted into college life well in his own way, both in work and play, but his ample resources and inclinations perhaps placed the emphasis too much on the latter.

By the end of the first year Yusupov invited his friend Eric Hamilton to stay with his family in St Petersburg. Hamilton's account of his remarkable visit provides a vivid snapshot of life in the rarified world of Russian high society. Beginning with Felix's enthusiastic greeting on arrival in St Petersburg, accompanied by *droshky* and 'vast coachman',[5] the young man was conveyed at a leisurely pace along the banks of the River Neva, past the Tsar's Winter Palace and the Hermitage, the British Embassy, and alongside St Mark's Cathedral to 94 Moika, the Yusupov Palace. It was to Hamilton

> … the biggest private house in the City and the most wonderful place of its kind I have ever seen. It is about the size of Buckingham Palace, with its own chapel and theatre complete with Royal Box, to say nothing of the huge ballroom and drawing room hung with the works of Raphael, Titian, Tiepolo, Rembrandt and other masters, ancient and modern.[6]

The rooms of the palace were decorated thematically, with a baroque theatre, Empire-style gala halls, a Turkish study and neo-classic ground-floor rooms. Furnished with an impressive collection of paintings, sculptures and tasteful furniture, it is still regarded as one of the most beautiful palaces in St Petersburg.

Two days after their arrival, Yusupov and Hamilton visited the Hermitage museum to study more Rembrandts and Rubens, only to find it closed. Hamilton recalled that 'Felix's name brought us through'.[7] Indeed the Yusupov name was to open many doors during the young Englishman's stay, as he visited the family's other equally impressive and palatial homes in far-flung parts of Russia. On one particularly memorable occasion, after lunch at Peterhof on the shores of the Gulf of Finland, where the Imperial family also had a vast residence, Hamilton was provided with a royal footman and car to take him to see Nicholas's palace. He was both amazed and delighted to find himself being 'motored back by the Tsar's private road along the sea front'.[8]

Moving on to Moscow, the students stayed at the Yusupov estate Arkhangelskoïe, about twenty miles outside the city, where Felix spent time at the grave of his brother Nicolas. A beautiful church in his memory was in mid-construction, although sadly it was never to be completed.

In the Crimea, where Hamilton visited the seaside 'eating grapes and peaches en route',[9] they called in at many of the estates of the Romanov grand dukes. A large party travelled in two cars to Balaclava on the way to Sebastopol, and Hamilton saw for himself 'with a thrill of pride, where the famous 600 of the Light Brigade charged down the valley with Lord Raglan at their head'.[10]

Towards the end of his stay in St Petersburg, Yusupov took Hamilton to the Fabergé emporium.

> The Prince told the chauffeur to stop outside their window, whose proprietor ran out with a small parcel which he handed to me. Without a thought I was passing it to Felix who waved it away, saying in his best English, 'Keep, keep'. To my confusion and amazement it contained a present of two large pearl studs.[11]

Back at Oxford, Felix Yusupov was about to enter his second year and he took accommodation outwith the college:

> I rented a very ordinary and unattractive little house in the town, which I quickly did up to suit me. Two of my fellow undergraduates, Jacques de Beistegui and Luigi Franchetti, came to live with me. The latter played the piano beautifully and we loved to listen to him till all hours of the night. I had brought a good chef from Russia. The rest of my staff was composed of a French chauffeur, an excellent English valet, Arthur Keeping, and a housekeeper and her husband who looked after three horses. I had brought a hunter and two polo ponies; a bulldog and a macaw completed my menagerie.[12]

Any individual with three horses, a title and unbelievable wealth would have been a natural guest at the Bullingdon, Oxford's most exclusive social club, and Yusupov was quick to join its ranks. In Victorian terms the Bullingdon was described as a sporting and dining club – or hunting, shooting and riding allied to excessive eating and drinking. With its distinctive uniform of Oxford blue and ivory tailcoat, with sky blue and ivory tie and mustard waistcoat, its popularity initially depended on opportunities it provided for riding out to Bullingdon Green where lavish dinners would be served. Photographs of past members still grace the walls of the King's Arms in Oxford, their excesses contributing to the club's lingering reputation.

If Yusupov's biggest triumph at Oxford was not related to academic achievement, his popularity was certainly assured when he used his influence to persuade Anna Pavlova to dance at the university theatre. On hearing that the organisers were friends of Yusupov, she readily agreed and brought the entire *corps de ballet* with her. Arriving at his rooms, she felt tired and took a nap on his bed while he escorted the company on a quick tour of the college. Alas, the parents of a girl Yusupov was alleged to have proposed to, chose that very moment to visit. Instead of Felix they found a world-famous ballerina asleep in his room. Yusupov, of course, was no longer pestered by the girl or her parents, and at the evening's performance he said, somewhat mischievously, 'Pavlova received a delirious ovation'.[13]

The arrival of the flamboyant Yusupov in England had not gone unnoticed in London society. Mrs Hwfa Williams was particularly quick to take him under her wing. Once described by Edward VII in the *New York Times* as Britain's best dressed woman, she was known for organising memorable social events, her dedication to entertaining often matched only by that of improving her social standing.[14] As Mrs Williams herself claimed:

> Throughout the week practically every night people were at a dinner party or a ball or the theatre or opera. I do not say we were busy in the daytime but there was always something to do and combined with a succession of late nights, the end of the week inevitably found me exhausted.[15]

The week did not stop there, however, as Felix Yusupov later confirmed:

> ... weekends at her house were always extremely gay. Her friends were all free and easy, sometimes a trifle questionable. They would turn up unexpectedly, and were always sure of a warm welcome at any time of the day or night, or might even find her ready to set off with them for an evening jaunt to London.[16]

Yusupov was similarly dedicated to excess. On one occasion, having been invited to a lavish fancy-dress ball at the Albert Hall, he ordered a Russian costume to be sent all the way from St Petersburg. It was made of gold brocade, embroidered with red flowers, studded with precious stones and edged with sable, and came with a *toque* to match. He was 'a sensation'.[17]

Yususpov once compared Mrs Williams to his macaw:

> [Mrs Williams] was very old and slightly deaf and as kind as as she could be. ... when she came to Felix's for dinner, [he] mischievously said, 'Mrs Hwfa, you know there's someone in London who looks just like Mary,' and he pointed to the macaw. 'Why! It's me!' Mrs Hwfa Williams said. ... 'Isn't [Felix] frightful!'[18]

For a succession of fancy-dress invitations, Yusupov acquired a set of costumes ranging from Louis XIV to a French sailor. He was also known to have made a spectacular entrance to a festivity at Earls Court organised by Jennie Cornwallis-West, arriving 'on a white horse covered with beautiful trappings'.[19]

Mrs Williams and Yusupov once arranged a masked dinner and dance together. According to Mrs Williams, 'we danced on till 3 am when a crowd of us went off in Felix's car, with his old bulldog Punch sitting on the front seat'. They ended up at Covent Garden in the early morning, watching the fruit arrive for market, 'discarding our masks on the way'.[20]

Yusupov had always been known for his unconventional, even risqué behaviour. Even before the untimely death of his brother, he admitted that his earlier youth had been full of dubious escapades. At twelve or thirteen, for example, he and a cousin had dressed up in women's clothes, including jewellery and wigs, and dined out at a fashionable restaurant. Before the champagne went to their heads, they had attracted the attention of a group of young officers.

On another evening a mistress of his brother agreed to escort Felix to a night club where gypsies provided the main entertainment. The mistress dressed her young charge as a woman and, as before, his disguise was very convincing. 'From that moment,' he later wrote, 'I began to lead a double life: by day I was a school boy and by night an elegant woman.'[21]

When staying in Paris, as they often did, Felix and Nicolas would sneak out undetected from their hotel in the Place Vendome by stepping over the ground floor window sill. One night, on finding out that there was to be a fancy-dress ball at the Opéra, they made plans to attend. Nicolas found himself a domino outfit, while Felix dressed once again in women's clothes. Before the ball they spent a few hours in costume, sitting in the front stalls of the Theatre des Capucines. 'After a while,' Felix said, 'I noticed that an old gentleman in a stage box was eyeing me persistently. When the lights went up for the interval I recognised King Edward VII.' Nicolas, he added, was accosted by a messenger at the interval, wanting to know, on behalf of His Majesty, the name of his lovely companion.[22]

Whether these stories are true or false may never be known. It is clear, however, that the habit of dressing up was a hard one to break, and when back in St Petersburg Yusupov claimed to have secured a job as a French woman singing fashionable Parisian songs at The Aquarium, one of the smartest *cafés-concert* in the city. He was, he said, quite a success. All went well until the seventh night when friends of his mother recognised him and the scandal broke. 'My career as a cabaret singer was nipped in the bud, but I did not give up the disguises which provided me with such delightful amusement.'[23]

Yusupov also claimed to have attended another ball in the Russian capital dressed in women's clothes, his face hidden behind a mask. There he was courted by a number of officers and persuaded to accompany them to a private room at a smart restaurant. When his mask was accidentally torn off, he made a swift exit. Throwing a bottle of champagne at a mirror, he flicked off the lights and fled into the night.

Felix himself hinted at a bisexual nature. When he was old enough to take an interest in women he freely admitted that 'life became even more complicated' and his attraction was always shortlived. 'Generally speaking I have found among men the loyalty and disinterestedness which I think most women lack.'[24]

After three years Yusupov left Oxford, but stayed on in London for a short time at a rented flat in Knightsbridge, just off Belgrave Square. It was there he met up with his cousin Prince Serge Obolensky who had just arrived from Russia to begin his first year at Christ Church, Oxford. Obolensky confessed he was not quite sure how they were related – first, second or third cousins? Nonetheless he was introduced as such to all of Yusupov's London friends, including Lady Gladys and Lady Juliet, Mrs Williams, Mrs John Jacob Astor (Serge's future mother-in-law) and, of course, Bertie Stopford.

Taken by Yusupov to his first London party at Mrs Williams' house at Coombe Springs, Obolensky soon became a regular guest there, and at nearby Coombe Court. Thus the young Russian found himself catapulted into the extravagant world of London high society, even before he had embraced the rigours of university life.

Born on 3 November 1890 in St Petersburg, Obolensky was the son of Platon Obolensky and Marie Narishkin. Having been accepted to read Political Economics, Poor Law and Local Government, Obolensky's first year at Oxford was to provide a remarkable contrast between slum clearances and low-cost housing, and social evenings with the London set in the occasional presence of royalty. Unlike cousin Felix, Obolensky was rather overwhelmed by it all:

> The social life of England's capital went on in an atmosphere unlike anything that I had seen or would ever see again anywhere in the world; I believe I saw the end of it. In those first years of the reign of George V, the mellow grandeur of the Edwardian age of art and conversation persisted, unquenched, uncompromising. In fact it was in full cry.[25]

Of course, not every first-year Oxford student received an invitation from Lady de Grey to attend a dinner in honour of Empress Maria of Russia and her sister Alexandra, the Queen Mother. The Empress had expressed a wish to meet Serge Obolensky who had been childhood friends with members of her own family. His father's work with blind people in Russia was administered through Marie's own benevolent association, and his uncle had been *haufmarschall* of her court. She was, nonetheless, genuinely interested in the young man's study of local government.

Obolensky, a liberal in outlook, took his academic work very seriously and slowly became attuned to the state of political affairs in Britain. He was to learn that

... progress was possible within the society that existed. In Russia my idealism was visionary and impractical, as was that of the reformers among my friends. ... in pre-war England I found that the hope of progress was recognised and accepted by all sides of society. ... [The reformers' thinking] was connected with practical work rather than with abstract ideas.[26]

Obolensky also took the opportunity to involve himself in student life. He joined the fencing club and dramatic society, rode to hounds, became a member of the Gridiron, an eating club, and, like Yusupov, enjoyed the excesses of the Bullingdon. He also played polo with the Prince of Wales, who had recently entered Magdalen College.

Obolensky's final end of term activity in the beautiful summer of 1914 was held at Hurlingham, where the Oxford polo team, with Serge as 'number one', played against Cambridge. They won by nineteen to one, Obolensky receiving his half blue. The defeat was too much for the Cambridge Old Boys who immediately challenged the young Oxford team to a return match next day. Whether the overnight celebrations undermined the Oxford men or not, they were duly trounced: 'The Old Cantabs rode around us all afternoon, scored at will, and made us look like beginners.'[27]

The next day, 28 June, Archduke Francis Ferdinand was assassinated in Sarajevo in far-off Bosnia. Though blissfully unaware at the time, the reverberations of that callous act were set to affect all the young men of Europe. Obolensky would never return to Oxford for his next term, and within a few short months he would be caught up in the war on the Eastern Front, riding with the Russian cavalry.

Felix Yusupov had already returned to Russia back in 1912. In St Petersburg he caught up with his long-time friend Grand Duke Dmitri Pavlovich, the son of Pavel Alexandrovich who was another uncle of the Tsar.

Pavel had been banished from the country by Nicholas when, after his first wife died, he entered into a morganatic marriage with his second wife Olga Pistolkors. In the absence of his father, Dmitri lived with an uncle, Sergei Alexandrovich, and his wife Elizaveta (Ella) Feodorovna, the sister of Tsarina Alexandra. After the death of Sergei at the hands of political revolutionaries in 1905, Elizaveta made plans to dedicate herself to a convent and Dmitri was taken under the wing of Nicholas and his family at the Alexander Palace.

The various scandals surrounding Yusupov's life had not gone unnoticed in court circles and Nicholas was worried about Dmitri's friendship with Felix. When the young men were witnessed out together in St Petersburg, enjoying the restaurants and night clubs in the company of Anna Pavlova and other members of the Imperial ballet, Nicholas put his foot down and forbade Dmitri to associate

with Felix. 'Inspectors of the secret police prowled around our house and followed me like a shadow when I went to St Petersburg,'[28] Yusupov complained. Neither Yusupov, Dmitri or Nicholas could have foreseen how disastrously entwined their lives would become in the not too distant future.

In 1913 Yusupov became reacquainted with a girl he had met many years before. Princess Irina Alexandrovna was the daughter of Grand Duchess Xenia, sister of the Tsar. He first encountered Irina when out riding on Koreitz, one of his family's estates in the Crimea. She made such an impression on the young man that he reined in his horse 'to gaze at her as she walked on'.[29] When Yusupov met her again

> … the child had grown into a girl of dazzling beauty. The deep feeling for her which was born in my heart made me realise the unworthiness and the triviality of my conduct in the past. … I concealed nothing in my past life from her and, far from being perturbed by what I told her, she showed great tolerance and comprehension.[30]

Her parents, and her grandmother Maria Feodorovna, were not quite so tolerant, and each insisted on quizzing Yusupov thoroughly about his intentions.

The couple were married on 22 February 1914 amid great splendour at the Anichkov Palace in St Petersburg, the home of Irina's grandmother. The bride arrived in a coach drawn by four white horses and was escorted into the ceremony on the arm of the Tsar himself.

The Yusupov nuptials turned out to be a last major fling of pre-war European society, with both Fabergé and Cartier drawn into the preparations. 'We were quite overwhelmed with gifts,' Yusupov wrote, '… the most gorgeous jewels as well as the simplest and most touching presents from our peasants.'[31] Irina's wedding veil had belonged to the ill-fated French queen Marie-Antoinette, and was lent to the bride by her mother. It was held in place by Felix's own gift – a special tiara of rock crystal and diamonds by Cartier.

The newlyweds enjoyed a leisurely tour of Paris, Egypt, Jerusalem, Italy and London – where they received the shocking news of Archduke Ferdinand's assassination. Travelling on to Germany as arranged, the couple found themselves temporarily stranded there at the outbreak of the war, and they were arrested by Kaiser Wilhelm in Berlin.

Escaping to Denmark on an Embassy train, the couple met up with Irina's mother and grandmother, Xenia and Empress Maria, whose own train had been attacked in Germany as they travelled back from London. From Denmark, the family caught a ferry bound for Sweden, before going on to Finland where the Imperial train was waiting to take them safely home to St Petersburg.

THE SHOCK OF WAR

(*Illustrated London News*, 4 December 1915)

CHAPTER SIX

At the Front

THE years before the First World War were, for those with wealth at least, a golden age. It was to make the shock of war when it arrived in August 1914 all the more difficult to accept. The contrast in fortunes was particularly obvious to the opera singer Nellie Melba. As an Australian guest at so many pre-war parties in London, she saw clearly what had been left behind. 'Perhaps had I been brought up in London,' she said later, 'I should not have noticed the glitter and the fantasy of that society at all.'

> It was not only an age of lovely women. It was a spacious age, when hospitality was far more lavish, probably, than it will ever be again. Who today, for example, would give a dinner party in which there was a pearl in each soup plate? And yet that was the way in which Hector Baltazzi celebrated his winning of the Derby.[1]

The London season had always been a challenge for the leading hostesses. Princess Marie Louise, in her book *My Memories of Six Reigns*, remembered it in this way:

> London society was brilliant. I might even say glamorous. ... balls, receptions, and of course large dinner parties took place every evening, and it was quite a usual occurrence to go to more than one ball the same night. ... There was no necessity to entertain outside one's own house, as in those days the Dorchester House, Grosvenor House, Landsdowne House, Derby House, Stafford House – all these beautiful residences were still inhabited by their owners. ... The aim of every Edwardian hostess, whether in town or country, was to be considered socially eminent. The most preferred occasion would have been a weekend house-party, entertaining King Edward VII and Queen Alexandra. Any weekend house-party demanded immense preparation, but a house-party that included Royalty taxed the hostess to her limit. Sumptuous food and twelve-course dinners were essential and shooting parties meant that lavish outdoor picnics were required.[2]

As the war progressed, the Princess recalled the last occasion she herself had organised, attended by both Lady Gladys de Grey and

Mrs Hwfa Williams. What brought home to her the tragic consequences of the conflict was the thought that of the twenty men who attended that evening in 1914, sixteen had been eligible for military service and ten were now dead. 'How well I remember Lady Juliet Duff and her husband Robin dancing together, with an expression of such happiness on their faces. He was one of the first to go.'[3]

Perhaps more surprising was the number of erstwhile party-givers who flung themselves into the war effort, setting up and supporting hospitals for the wounded at home and abroad. Lady Gladys and Lady Muriel Paget became involved almost immediately. So too did the Duchess of Sutherland, who organised a hospital in Belgium under the auspices of the Red Cross, using financial backing from American friends. Albert Stopford also made himself available to offer assistance and was soon working alongside them, originally from his base in Paris and later close to the Front in Belgium.

Voluntary work aside, it remains far from clear what precise role Stopford had found for himself at the beginning of the war. He has since been described variously as a King's messenger, diplomatic or war courier, intelligence agent, and even a member of the somewhat shadowy British Secret Service Bureau formed in 1909. Whatever his occupation, details of his activities as they emerge from this time reveal that he was somehow able to win the confidence of influential people at all levels, including military leaders, foreign ministers, and members of the security services.

In the first month of the conflict, Stopford watched and waited with the rest of Paris as the German armies moved quickly through Belgium and France, emerging as a threat to the city itself. As the German advance progressed, people began to leave. Paris was virtually deserted. The tourists were gone; the hotels were either empty or had, like the Hotel Meurice, been turned into military hospitals. Civilian traffic dried up as vehicles were commandeered for the war effort. The historian Barbara Tuchman summed up the atmosphere in the city: 'For one August in its history Paris was French – and silent.'[4] The authorities now debated whether to defend the capital or to declare it an open city.

Parisians followed the Allied response to the early German advances with increasing anxiety. Although the battle of Mons had brought part of the advance to a halt, the French Army was desperate to bring some semblance of stability to the front line and to find a natural barrier to defend. The river Marne was an obvious choice and Paris was put under the direct control of General Gallieni, the Military Governor. Lacking sufficient transport to move reserve troops up to the battlefront, Gallieni called upon the service of Parisian taxi-cabs. By his calculation, with one hundred already commandeered, an extra five hundred taxis would enable the transport of six thousand additional troops to the Front. The drivers were given five hours to assemble and, despite the odds, managed to meet the deadline. Whether or not the swift movement of extra troops proved significant enough to sway the outcome of the first battle on the Marne, the action plainly raised morale in the capital at a crucial early stage of the war, and this important Allied victory ended the month-long offensive that opened the conflict.

The battle itself raged for nearly a week, after which the German command began to pull back. Paris braced itself for the first flood of casualties arriving at the hospitals – French and British as well as German. The military hospital, Hopital du Val de Grace on the Left Bank, was the main recipient. Albert Stopford watched the return of the injured soldiers:

> The Germans had retreated, leaving their wounded on the field. General Gallieni, with characteristic kindness, had them all brought to Paris. At that time I was going every day to the Val de Grace Hospital to see the English wounded, who were being brought in with the French.[5]

The focus of the war swiftly moved to the Channel Ports, as the German armies swung westwards. Several of London's society ladies were already helping to set up field hospitals nearer the Front, among them some of Stopford's friends including the Duchess of Sutherland, Lady Gladys, Lady Juliet Duff and Lady Sarah Wilson. Lady Muriel Paget had already been involved in charitable work since 1905, organising invalid kitchens in Southwark in south London. Stopford, having followed the ebb and flow of fighting to the Channel Ports, offered his support as they planned an expansion of field hospitals behind Allied lines.[6]

By 1915 there was an urgent need for these field hospitals to care for the increasing number of casualties as the British Expeditionary Force undertook a difficult, strategic retreat along the French coast. To assist the military operation, medical resources were deployed between Antwerp, Ostend and Boulogne. Stopford was involved in hospital liaison work by this time, working near the front lines, especially around Ypres. Despite the very real dangers that surrounded him, he remained remarkably unscathed, apart from an accident involving a motor-car during the swift evacuation of Ostend.

Amid the terrible carnage witnessed at the hospitals there was a rather incongruous event that Stopford later recalled. Lady Gladys de Grey had been determined that the wounded men should be kept entertained during the first Christmas of the war and she secured no less than sixty-six pianos from friends and acquaintances, on the strict understanding that they would be returned the following day.

For Lady Gladys, morale was just as important as medicine for the war effort.

Stopford himself was also no stranger to morale-boosting efforts. He claimed that he crossed the Channel seventy-eight times during a three-month period in the early part of the war, bringing back gifts for British soldiers recovering in Allied institutions and hospitals. Travelling regularly back and forth from England at this time, it is thought that Stopford acted as a personal messenger for Queen Mary on at least one occasion, although nothing is known about the content of any messages carried.

Not long after the field hospitals were established on the Western Front, thoughts turned to the possibility of extending similar strategic support services to the Eastern Front. Lady Muriel had been alerted to the need for such facilities by Professor Bernard Pares of the University of Liverpool, who invited her to join a society with a particular interest in Russia. Lady Muriel decided that a unit of English surgeons and nurses should be sent to Russia as a gesture of goodwill and began by setting down some practical proposals. First she secured the backing of the Russian Ambassador and British Foreign Secretary, and a committee was set up. Lord Cromer, the former Consul-General in Egypt, was appointed as its president, with Queen Alexandra, the sister of the Russian Empress Maria Feodor-

BRITISH SOLDIERS AT BOULOGNE

Wounded soldiers watch a variety show that was toured to various hospital premises in a bid to keep up morale.

(*The War Illustrated*, volume II, Winter 1914)

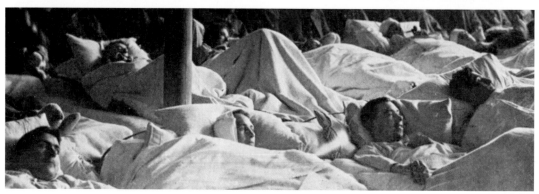

ovna, as patron. With King George and Queen Mary at the top of the subscription list, the idea behind the Anglo-Russian Hospital began to take shape.

The hospital's organisers were persuaded that a base hospital in the Russian capital would be a more practical venture given the fluid situation on the Eastern Front, so Lady Muriel began the project by visiting hospitals in Boulogne to identify practical problems and solutions. She then persuaded businesses to provide equipment, and began a round of interviews in London with medical staff.

In the meantime, sites in St Petersburg were assessed for suitability. The palace of Grand Duke Dmitri Pavlovich, situated on the corner of the Nevsky Prospect and Fontanka Canal, was eventually selected, as the spacious ballrooms and reception rooms would provide an ideal layout for wards and treatment rooms. Dmitri was introduced to the venture through Stopford and Felix Yusupov, and readily agreed to the palace being used.

Following his involvement in the siting of the Anglo-Russian Hospital, the decision-makers at Whitehall must have realised that Albert Stopford might be of further use to them in Russia, where his contacts in the Tsarist court were at such a high level.

For Stopford this marked the beginning of more than two long years of travel to and from Russia; and of a personal journey that would take him thousands of miles within that vast Empire.

CHAPTER SEVEN

Petrograd

44

Saxe Coburg Gotha

BY the beginning of the war, anti-German feeling in Russia had been running so high that the German-sounding name St Petersburg was altered to the Russian Petrograd, and it remained so until 1924 when it became known as Leningrad. It was much the same sentiment that led the British Royal family to change their name from ~~Battenburg~~ to Windsor in 1917.

Albert Stopford had visited St Petersburg on a couple of occasions before the war, and in March 1914 he stayed in room 157 at the luxurious Hôtel de l'Europe, using it as a base to develop his business activities and to catch up with friends.

On Sunday 18 July 1915 [New Style calendar (N.S.)],[*] Stopford was back in the Russian capital yet again, and had booked himself into the same room at the Hôtel de l'Europe. As this would prove to be an extended visit, he kept a diary of his time in Russia which was later published as *The Russian Diary of an Englishman: Petrograd, 1915-1917*.[1]

Three days later Stopford took Colonel C. B. Thomson, the British Military Attaché, to lunch with Maria Pavlovna at her palace in Tsarskoe Selo outside Petrograd. Having just returned from attending church with her nephew Tsar Nicholas,[2] Maria arranged for the food to be served in a tent in the garden where she often took lunch during the summer months. It was one of many such meetings between Stopford and Maria, offering the opportunity for a leisurely exchange of news and gossip, and it was not long before Stopford took to telephoning the Grand Duchess whenever he had something of interest to discuss.

One person who benefited from this special relationship was the British Ambassador to Russia, Sir George Buchanan, who, with his wife, accompanied Stopford to meet the Grand Duchess only a week later. Buchanan was an archetypal Englishman and bore all the trappings of a professional diplomat. He was certainly no fool and inspired trust in those who knew him, including the Tsar himself. His wife Lady Georgina was a very generous and kind-hearted lady, and Stopford came to know well during his stay in Petrograd.

*NOTE ON DATES

Until 1918 Russia adhered to the earlier Julian calendar [Old Style or O.S.] of 365.25 days and was 13 days behind the rest of Europe which followed the later Gregorian calendar. In February 1918, Russia adopted the Gregorian calendar and omitted or jumped 13 days. As Stopford's diary was written using the Gregorian calendar [New Style or N.S.], this will be used for this and subsequent references based on his diary entries, unless otherwise indicated.

If the diary is any indication, Stopford appeared be in his element in Petrograd, quickly reviving old friendships in his usual congenial manner. A few months after his arrival in the city he was dining on the roof of his hotel with Tamara Karsavina from the *Ballets Russes*. Karsavina had just accompanied him to see a doctor, acting as his interpreter. 'We had to wait an hour,' Stopford wrote, 'and then, while she held my hand, the doctor shoved things through my nose! … It was good of her and I am much touched.'[3]

Stopford was acutely aware that he was in a foreign country, although an allied state, without a formal title or military uniform. He was not listed among the staff of the British Embassy or Foreign Office, or classed as a King's messenger, and he held no rank in any of the armed services. Although he had 'understandings' with White-hall and the British Government, and enjoyed access to the Embassy and diplomatic services in Petrograd, he seemed to be acting independently. With his connections, however – particularly with the influential Grand Duchess Maria Pavlovna – he had found a way to open doors all the way to the top and to create a unique, if unofficial, role for himself during the war.

45

PETROGRAD, *c.*1910

People going about their daily business on the well-known thoroughfare of Nevsky Prospect.

(Library of Congress)

Settling into the Hôtel de l'Europe in July 1915 Stopford observed that the atmosphere in the Russian capital was similar to that in Paris and Boulogne the previous autumn. Although the Russian Army had gained earlier successes, particularly on the Austrian Front and even in Eastern Prussia, as the war raged on through 1915 one reverse after another was inflicted upon the Tsar's forces. By the end of the first six months Russia had lost almost a million soldiers – killed, wounded or missing in action – and a catastrophic capitulation of Russian-held Poland, Lithuania and Latvia soon followed. The cities of Kiev and Riga were now under threat, and so was Petrograd itself.

As a reflection of the growing anxiety within the city, but also because the Tsar's Winter Palace had been partly turned into a hospital, the crown jewels, small *objets d'art* and Imperial plate from Petrograd and Warsaw were moved to the Kremlin in Moscow for safety. Nine large strong-boxes were used to move the Grand Imperial crown, sceptre and orb, and other state regalia from the House of Fabergé, where they were in the process of being re-catalogued.

Stopford wrote on 22 August 1915 to Lady Sarah Wilson, a friend working at the Allied Forces Hospital in Boulogne:

> We have been going through here exactly the same emotions as you and I went through together last year in Paris and Boulogne. I never thought such an experience could happen twice in one's life. We all expect the Germans here sooner or later. Till Riga falls no one will know whether their [objective] is Petrograd or Moscow; if Petrograd, their Fleet could co-operate with them. The major part of the artillery and munitions are here.
>
> On the other hand, it is calculated that it would take them six weeks to get here, and the winter usually begins in about six weeks' time. The snow that made Napoleon pack up next morning fell on October 12. Pray God it may be an early winter!
>
> If they do come here, will there be a revolution? The fear is that *people* might rise and make peace to stop the German advance, feeling that the Romanovs have had their chance and been found wanting.[4]

As he was now involved in the setting up of the Anglo-Russian Hospital, Stopford set out to investigate what was already being done by the Russian authorities for the casualties of the war on the Eastern Front. His first visit, on 31 August, was to the British Colony Hospital, where he spoke with some of the Russian casualties. He later noted in his diary that 'of the eighty-two wounded there, over forty are on crutches, shot in the legs during retreat. ... A Cossack was playing his guitar in the garden, and there were nine legs listening with eighteen brains!'[5] Stopford was back at the same hospital a week later with Lady Georgina, after attending the King George the Fifth

Hospital on the Nevsky Prospect. He was a popular visitor, as he kept a constant supply of small gifts about his person, especially cigarettes. Lady Georgina was involved in the distribution of clothing for outgoing troops and their families, which was desperately needed.

On 2 October Lady Georgina asked Stopford to accompany her to Petrograd's Warsaw Station to help with 'bath trains' that she had secured from the station master. These were being equipped with vapour baths and drying rooms, ready to be sent to the Front for the troops. The trains also provided temporary washing facilities for children at a nearby home for Polish refugees. Stopford helped to bathe the children – 'two howled'[6] – and went back the following week to do it all over again. But as if to underline the rather odd contrast in his activities, he also took time to purchase some caviar for Lord Kitchener, the British Secretary of State for War, and get it over to the British Embassy to be forwarded to London.

The next day Stopford could be found at the Town Hospital for Soldiers, again giving away cigarettes. Strict good manners were always observed. In each ward the accompanying Russian officer Colonel Schahovskoi called out, 'Your English brother brings you these [cigarettes]!', to which the wounded shouted back 'Most humbly we thank him'. 'To one poor man looking very ill I gave a packet,' Stopford wrote. 'With beautiful manners he said, "Thank you," and then turned over and died.'[7]

Later, the Colonel was kind enough to drive Stopford out to Princess Putiatin's Hospital for Officers, where the Tsarina and two of her daughters, Olga and Tatiana, were involved in hospital work.

As the German advance continued on the Eastern Front, the return of wounded to the capital grew steadily, and the need for ambulance trains increased. Maria Pavlovna had organised and financed an ambulance train back in 1905, the first of its kind, during the Russo-Japanese War. It was followed by five more, paid for by the Tsarina and her daughters. By 1915 there were three hundred. As a special favour to Stopford, Maria smuggled him on board one of her trains during a visit to the Front in November. The arduous thirty-hour journey took them beyond Dvinsk, over three hundred miles south-west of the capital, coming to a halt within three miles of the fighting. Stopford once again witnessed the terrible reality of war:

> It was a weird sight as we went out of the station with torches to meet the wounded, who were being brought in by peasants in carts; there were only a few motor-ambulances as the roads are indescribably bad; many of the men were undressed, and the carts were dripping with blood. It must have been like that in Napoleon's time – the same place and time of the year. But once the poor things were in the train there was every comfort and luxury.[8]

Two trains of twenty-nine carriages made the return journey, loaded up with almost five hundred wounded soldiers. Stopford and Maria visited each one in turn, offering comfort and cigarettes. Mlle Olive, Maria's attendant and Stopford's friend, sat with the dying. '[They] went out like watches run-down, without effort … [They] just stopped breathing.'[9]

The experience was to prove invaluable to Stopford with the official opening of the Anglo-Russian Hospital set for February 1916, and he was gratified to know that Maria Pavlovna was not the only member of the Russian Imperial family to show an interest in the project. Back in October 1915, the Empress Maria and Tsarina Alexandra had received a deputation from the hospital's senior staff, and promises had been made to attend the opening. With the Empress Maria and Grand Duchesses Olga and Tatiana Nicholaevna present on the day, Russian royal support could not have been greater.

Lady Muriel Paget was due to arrive in Petrograd in May 1916. Although she and Stopford had met before on social occasions (she was one of his guests at the Savoy just before the war), it was the first time he had spent any length of time in her company. Stopford found himself impressed by her energy and the way she channelled it into the Anglo-Russian Hospital project, making it 'more human and more useful'.[10]

With Lady Muriel having additional plans to set up a field hospital at the Russian Front, similar to the ones in France, Stopford suggested a visit to Maria Pavlovna. With her long-term experience of ambulance trains, the Grand Duchess would be of enormous help. When the two women met, Lady Muriel outlined her intention to create a hospital unit attached to the Guards division. Within minutes, Maria's son Andrei had telephoned the regiment to set up a meeting with the general in charge.

Stopford's connections appeared to be working well, and the Anglo-Russian Hospital benefited from his efforts, but his own personal contribution to the wider British war effort remained vague. His 'work' seemed to involve socialising with members of the Russian aristocracy, an endless round of meetings at embassies and war offices, attending the opera or ballet, or travelling between Petrograd and London. But all the time Stopford was developing his contacts at the Tsarist court, reviving old friendships with the likes of Felix Yusupov, Serge Obolensky and the family of Maria Pavlovna. When he was ready to extend his network, he began with one of his earliest introductions in Petrograd, Count Paul Benckendorff, Marshal of the Imperial Court and brother of the Russian Ambassador in London. Benckendorff was in charge of the Tsar's personal finances and, as such, a very useful contact indeed. Through him Stopford met Prince Michael Putiatin who provided him with a pass to attend services at the Feodorovsky Sobor, the cathedral in Tsarskoe Selo attended by the Tsar and his family. This gave Stopford an unrivalled opportunity to observe the Imperial family in a more informal setting.

The value of these special court contacts became apparent within three months of Stopford's arrival in Petrograd, when he began to hear rumours that all was not well between Russian Army command and the Tsar. As the German Army made advances along the Eastern Front, the Russians were forced to pull back. Boris Vladimirovich, a Hussar on active service, told Stopford 'heart-rending accounts of the retreat; of the Russians burning their own villages'.[11] As the number of casualties escalated and communication from Nicholas's Commander-in-Chief, Grand Duke Nicholas Nicholaevich, became strained, the Imperial family's confidence in their military leaders began to waver.

The Tsarina did not particularly like Nicholas Nicholaevich, even though he was a member of the family. In 1905 he had refused to establish a military dictatorship to quell revolutionary uprisings, and the Tsar had been forced to accept political reform instead. This went against Alexandra's rigidly-held belief in the absolute power of autocratic rule; and as an influential voice in her husband's ear she made her antipathy towards Nicholaevich perfectly clear. But would the notoriously indecisive Tsar take the difficult decision to sack his experienced Commander-in-Chief? And if so, who would take over?

The answer came on 3 September. Stopford had been invited to dine with Maria Pavlovna at Tsarskoe Selo, and he arrived punctually at six o'clock at the Vladimir Palace alongside the River Neva to wait for a lift. Karl Fabergé, known to Stopford from his dealings in *objets d'art*, was already there, patiently waiting for their hostess. Maria eventually arrived three-quarters of an hour late, 'full of apologies and looking very worried'. Stopford was taken aback, as 'no Romanov has ever been known to be late for dinner'.[12] As they were being motored out of the city, Maria remained quiet and distracted.

The Grand Duchess had been with the Maria Feodorovna that afternoon. At Tsarskoe Selo, over 'lukewarm potage St-Germain',[13] she mentioned in the passing that Nicholas and Alexandra had been to Tsar Alexander's tomb to pray that day. Then she dropped the bombshell.

> The Emperor leaves to-morrow night, to take over the Supreme Command at the Front. [Nicholas Nicholaevich] goes to the Caucasus. ... It is quite disastrous.[14]

The news was indeed disastrous. The Tsar, who was not experienced in military matters, would now take full responsibility for any future military failures. But of more concern to the running of the country, Nicholas's absence from Petrograd would inevitably create a political vacuum. With the Tsar based over three hundred miles away at the Military Headquarters (*Stavka*) in Moghilev, the Tsarina Alexandra and certain other individuals at court would be left to influence important decisions of state in the capital. Maria Pavlovna was devastated.

Stopford did not lose sight of the gravity of this news for the Allies in London and Paris and he went immediately to the British Embassy to inform Lord Buchanan, who had not yet been made aware of the Tsar's decision. 'The Ambassador thanked me very much,'[15] Stopford wrote, with barely concealed pride.

* * *

By the spring of 1916 Stopford had established a whole new network of contacts within Russian ministries and embassies, occasionally using his friends at court to ensure a smooth introduction. He first met Sergei Sazanov, the current Russian Minister for Foreign Affairs, when he visited St Petersburg before the war. Sazanov was a popular man who was well respected by Russian and Allied personnel alike, and Stopford felt privileged to dine with him on a regular basis.

Stopford was also introduced to the former Minister of War, Vladimir Sukhomlinov, and later to Admiral Ivan Grigorovich, the Minister of Marine. His military contacts also included General Lukomski at the War Office, Sir John Hanbury-Williams, head of the British Military Mission at the Russian Military Headquarters, as well as a number of military attaches who moved through the capital, some already known to him from Paris.

These new contacts provided Stopford with access to military camps across the country, and in March 1916 he travelled south by train to visit a Cossack outfit in Tiflis, beyond the Caucasus. Major-General Sir Charles Callwell, who was primarily in Russia to discuss munition supplies on behalf of the British War Office, was also there. Callwell, a friend of Lord Kitchener, had been asked to go to Tiflis to honour the Russian Commander Nikolai Yudenich who had taken Erzrumn on 16 February from the Turkish forces. This was to prove an important strategic victory, as Russia now controlled all the roads to the Black Sea.

Boris Vladimirovich was also proving to be useful for military contacts. He took Stopford to meet the head of the Russian Air Service in Kiev, and later introduced him to General Count Gregor von Nostitz in Finland. Stopford's access to key Allied military personnel was impressive for a mere civilian.

Since his arrival in Petrograd, Stopford had dined regularly at the

French Embassy where he knew many individuals from his time in Paris. M. Crupi, the former French Minister of Foreign Affairs, was already known to him, and he was likewise acquainted with Maurice Paleologue, the French Ambassador, and his deputy M. Thomas. On his trips back to London Stopford would often stop off in Paris to pass messages to and from the French Embassy in Petrograd.

Stopford had need to use his connections to extricate himself from an awkward situation at the Customs post on the Finnish-Russian border. On 21 January 1916, returning from a month-long trip to London, he was asked to show what he was carrying in the 'Foreign Office bag':

> … I had passed out of France into England, out of England into Norway, out of Norway into Sweden, and out of Sweden, without any examination. I protested that, as I was carrying a Foreign Office bag, English and French official papers, and letters from the Russian Embassy, I would not allow anything to be touched now that I was in Russia. The head official replied, 'You are in Finland, not Russia!' On my declaring that I would sit on my luggage until orders arrived personally from the Minister for Foreign Affairs in Petrograd, they climbed down.[16]

Two weeks after his return from London, Stopford found out that the Tsar was back from Moghilev and he used his pass to attend the Feodorovsky cathedral. 'I shall go on Sunday just to see the Emperor smile and hear the Cossacks salute him with a yell!'[17] But Stopford had an ulterior motive for wanting to see the Imperial family, for he had just penned a memorandum to the Tsar requesting an audience. By the time Stopford had met with Maria Pavlovna that week, Boris had helpfully passed his letter on to the right quarters.

A day later Stopford was informed that 'official approval had already been telegraphed by the Emperor's command'.[18] The British Embassy telephoned him to say – 'laconically', Stopford thought – that 'the Emperor will receive you at half-past two to-morrow'.[19]

Albert Stopford, a foreigner, with no official status, had been granted an opportunity to meet with the supreme commander of the Russian Army, the man known as the 'Tsar of all the Russias', on what appeared to be a private matter. It was unthinkable.

By chance Stopford was dining at the French Embassy that evening. Boris had also been invited, and he advised his friend to 'talk to the Emperor just as you do to me, and tell him everything you know'.[20] Boris had already spoken with Nicholas about Stopford, and Sergei Sazanov had put in a good word. The French Ambassador simply told him to keep talking! *Ne laissez tomber jamais la conversation.*[21]

The British Embassy however was bemused. Stopford's invitation was 'unique'. The Embassy had no influence with the Tsar to request a meeting with a private British subject. They could not even advise him on sartorial matters. But Stopford had no need to worry, as officials of the Imperial court instructed him on correct dress code, and arranged for a carriage to collect him from the railway station at Tsarskoe Selo. On his arrival at the Alexander Palace, he was escorted to a special suite to wait for his meeting.

Stopford learned from a courtier that Maria Pavlovna had just been to lunch with Nicholas and Alexandra. She later said that she had taken the opportunity to mention him to the Tsar. Nicholas had even suggested that Alexandra might like to receive Stopford, but the Tsarina was already committed to a hospital visit. Stopford later said that he was secretly glad of this, as her presence would have shortened his time with the Tsar.

How far this paving of the way influenced the nature of the interview is impossible to know, but from Stopford's own account it turned out to be a relaxed affair. In contrast to reports that audiences were normally given standing up and lasted little more than ten minutes, the Tsar pointed to a seat and offered him a cigarette. Nicholas said that he was glad Stopford could make their meeting that day, as he was due to leave for the Front that night. It was, he said rather revealingly, 'the most agreeable of all my duties'.[22]

Nicholas thought he recognised Stopford.

> 'I know your face; I think we must have met before.'
>
> [Stopford] replied, 'I think sir, you may have seen me at the Feodorovski Sobor [cathedral], as I have permission to attend your Majesty's Church'. His simplicity wins one's heart.[23]

The Tsar spoke about his son Alexei and his current state of health, and mentioned that his mother missed her sister Alexandra in Britain very much. He said the Empress's train had been attacked as it travelled through Germany just after the war broke out. He would never forgive the German people for their ill-treatment of his mother.

Adept at polite conversation, the Tsar remembered an occasion in 1896 when in London, he accompanied Queen Victoria to visit a near relative of Stopford. (The relative in question was probably Stopford's Aunt Horatia.)

Stopford took the opportunity to explain why he had requested this audience. Although significantly he provides no details in his diary, it was later revealed that he was carrying personal correspondence from King George V.

When the conversation returned to the war, and 'America, Zeppelins, munitions … and God knows what!',[24] Stopford told Nicholas about his own experiences in France and Belgium:

... the exodus from Paris ... the Battle of the Marne ... my automobile accident at the evacuation of Ostend ... my visit to Ypres. ...
I related how Lady Ripon, in the King George the Fifth Hospital,
with her wonderful instinct for organisation, got hold of sixty-six
pianos ... for the wounded soldiers' entertainment at Christmas. ...[25]

Nicholas talked of Lord Kitchener and assured Stopford that the
British Secretary of State for War was well respected in the Russian
Army. 'We should all feel it deeply if he were to leave the War Office,'
Nicholas said. He also hoped that General Callwell, whose com-
pany he enjoyed, would be back in Petrograd soon, 'with lots of news
and other things'.[26]
Nicholas asked where Stopford was staying in Petrograd.

I named my hotel, and he remarked, 'I believe there's a newer hotel,
but I can't remember the name.' I said the new hotel was the rendez-
vous of a not very attractive clientele. He laughed – 'Perhaps you are
getting old?' I rejoined, 'No sir! It's the ladies that are old; I still feel
quite young.'[27]

As Stopford took his leave, Nicholas, no doubt mindful of the
private message he had just received from London through this
enigmatic Englishman, turned to him and said: 'If you leave without
my seeing you again, please convey to the King and Queen that I
am always thinking of them, and lay all my affectionate love at their
feet.'[28]
Two weeks later, one of the personal messages Stopford had passed to the Tsar was revealed as the British sovereign's recognition of
Nicholas II as Russia's new Commander-in-Chief. Stopford was
present at the British Embassy when General Sir Arthur Paget and
Lord Pembroke, who had made the journey specially to Petrograd,
handed over a British Field-Marshal's baton to the Tsar from King
George V as a token of his respect. The news of the appointment,
which Stopford had brought from London to Petrograd, was concluded with a congratulatory message from Buckingham Palace to
His Imperial Majesty.
The event, albeit a minor one amid the turmoil of the war, only
served to enhance the standing of Albert Stopford where it mattered.

PETROGRAD, 1917

A military barricade set up in the streets of Petrograd
during the early days of the Revolution, from a newspaper article dated 21 April 1917.

(*Illustrated London News*)

CHAPTER EIGHT

Rasputin and Revolution

A LTHOUGH it remains difficult to assess exactly what kind of work Stopford was engaged in during his time in Petrograd, his diary, along with letters to his friends, points to someone acting as eyes and ears for the Allied authorities. His main sources were his friends, many of whom were royalty or nobility, but his network had extended to include many officials, generals and ministers involved in the administration of the war effort on the Eastern Front. With his self-effacing manner and meticulous attention to detail, he solicited information very efficiently.

Stopford realised that accurate news of the Russian war effort could never be obtained from the British Embassy. 'Any news that comes to me from the Embassy – and they are most kind – consists only of the official Russian bulletins which appear later in the Press; so I have taken other steps to keep myself informed.'[1] These 'steps' involved regular meetings with those in the know, and his diary often reads like a who's who with its impressive list of lunches and dinners with diplomats, military men, Romanovs and foreign correspondents. It was not all one-sided, however, as Stopford appeared to be as useful to his sources as they were to him. His quid pro quo approach worked very effectively, with Maria Pavlovna an especially rich source for much that was going on in the capital.

During his first few months in Petrograd, Stopford's attention had focused on the losses inflicted upon the Russian Army as it became clear that all was far from well at the top. From what he had witnessed in person at the Front, he could see that Russian military leaders had much to answer for. 'It's terrible, the bungling inefficiency of the Staff,' Stopford wrote at the end of August 1915. 'The Soldiers are beyond all praise.'[2]

Resources were completely inadequate, and even when munitions were available, distribution was hindered by transport problems.

At the end of 1914 with the initial mobilisation completed, Russia had under arms 6.5 million men, but only 4.6 million rifles. To meet these shortages and compensate for combat losses, the army required each month a minimum of 100,000 to 50,000 rifles, but Russian industry could at best provide only 27,000. ... Also in relation to her territory, Russia fell far behind the other main belligerents: whereas for each 100 square kilometres, Germany had 10.6 kilometres of railways, France 8.8, and Austria-Hungary 6.4, Russia had a mere 1.1. This was one of the major reasons for the slowness of her mobilisation.[3]

The roots of Russia's growing social unrest went far back into the history of the Empire and the changing policies of successive Tsars. When Alexander III came to power in 1881, he was an uncompromising ruler. His father, the more liberally-minded Alexander II, had been cruelly assassinated by a terrorist's bomb; and for his son, censorship, secret police, restrictions on education, and the persecution of non-Russians in the Empire, became his trademark policies. In an attempt to overturn the liberal reforms introduced by his father, his main adviser Konstantin Pobedonostsev, a staunch believer in autocratic rule, did all that he could to enforce the Russian way of life on the inhabitants of that vast and diverse Empire.

When Nicholas II ascended the throne in 1894 he was determined to rule as his father had, and relied on Konstantin Pobedonostsev until he retired. Nicholas also retained Sergei Yulyevich Witte, his father's trusted Minister of Finance, who looked towards economic modernisation and Russia's integration with Europe as fundamental to its future growth. Taking advice from such opposing policymakers, however, would inevitably lead to conflict, and the rule of Tsar Nicholas was to prove fatally inconsistent.

Pobedonostsev's reforms in the countryside, which favoured the land-owning classes, led to serious outbreaks of violence between the peasants and their landlords, and the peasants turned to a new political group, the Social Revolutionary Party, for support. At the same time, the liberal, middle-class leaders of the local *zemstvos* or councils, who wished to improve the conditions of the peasants, were also following their own agenda for parliamentary reform with the creation of a League of Liberation. During the first decade of the twentieth century, these two groups moved closer together to demand an end to autocratic rule.

Under Sergei Witte, the industrialisation of the country was gathering pace as he sought to gain a foothold among leading Western economies. To increase productivity, railways had been built – the most politically significant being the Trans-Siberian line. By 1901 the route had been engineered from Moscow to the Russian port of Vladivostock on the Pacific coast. To avoid a six-hundred mile detour around Chinese territory, Russia had persuaded China to allow the line to cross Manchuria. When Russia leased Port Arthur from the Chinese to provide a more accessible port than Vladivostock during the harsh winters, the railway line was further extended.

But the progress of the Trans-Siberian railway alarmed Japan, who occupied Korea on the border of Manchuria. When Japan tried diplomacy in the first instance to avoid conflict, some of the Tsar's ministers were less than polite. They had ulterior motives. The unpopularity of recent land reforms and the expansion of industrialisation in Russia had come at the expense of the working classes, the proletariat, and an increasing number of highly organised political protests and bloody terrorist campaigns were beginning to disrupt the running of the country. A small war, easily won, might avert unrest at home.

On 8/9 February 1904 [N.S.] Japanese boats launched a surprise attack on the Russian fleet in Port Arthur, declaring war the next day. Russia immediately responded, but its high command had miscalculated the military strength of Japan. Over a period of a year and a half Port Arthur was to fall and the Russian Army was forced out of Manchuria. When the second Russian Pacific Fleet reached the Sea of Japan in May 1905, it was destroyed by the Japanese Navy in the Straits of Tsushima. A peace treaty was finally signed on 5 September 1905, mainly due to the conciliatory efforts of Sergei Witte.

But it had been a humiliating defeat that angered the people of Russia. Their forces had been ill-prepared and badly, even cruelly, led. Many had seen the conduct of the war as proof of the Tsar's ineffectual leadership at best and corruption at worst.

The defeat also followed in the wake of the terrible events of 9 January 1905 [O.S.]. With continuing losses against Japan affecting the prevailing mood in the country, resentment towards the harsh economic conditions endured by Russia's peasants had led to crowds of St Petersburg workers gathering in protest in front of the Winter Palace, the Imperial family's main residence. There they demanded an end to the war against Japan, and democracy in government. When the Tsar's troops opened fire on the people, killing hundreds of innocent civilians and wounding many more, peaceful protest escalated into a series of angry strikes. The tragedy later became known as 'Bloody Sunday'.

Disturbances rippled throughout the country as factions within the Socialist Revolutionaries increased their campaign of terrorism. Landlords were attacked and killed, sailors on the battleship *Potemkin* mutinied, and the army and navy, still engaged in battle against the Japanese, teetered on the brink of collapse. In Moscow the Tsar's uncle, Sergei Alexandrovich, was assasinated. Soon the ranks of the protesters were swelled by students, doctors and teachers, and councils (*soviets*) of workers were set up to represent trades and factories. The socialists and liberals had become a formidable force.

In St Petersburg a powerful Soviet of Workers' Deputies was formed, with Leon Trotsky among its number. Trotsky, initially a supporter of the *Menshevik* group of the Russian Social Democratic Labour Party, believed that the future of Russia lay with its workers and trade unions, a view that was held by many as the *soviets* throughout the country took over the leadership of the strikes.

With such a groundswell of opinion in favour of change, the demands for public representation in government had become difficult to resist. Forced into reluctant submission by the liberals among his ministers, including Sergei Witte, Nicholas agreed in October 1905 to grant a constitution, promising to share power with a legislative body and to honour civil liberties. To achieve this, a Russian parliament or *duma* was created, based at the Tauride Palace in St Petersburg.

The Duma ran from April 1906, with Sergei Witte as its first Prime Minister, but it was hardly a parliamentary legislature as understood in the West. Although the Duma gave members the right to free speech, the Tsar retained the right to appoint and dismiss ministers, and to declare war and make peace. The membership was made up of liberals (the Constitutional Democratic [Cadet] Party), and Social Revolutionaries led by intellectuals but supported by peasants. The Social Democrats – the *Mensheviks* and the more radical *Bolsheviks* led by Vladimir Ilyich Ulyanov (known as Lenin) – refused to take part in the elections.

The overwhelming majority of the Tsar's new parliament was not on his side, however, and from the outset he found himself in a constant battle between the liberal and socialist factions within its ranks, determined to extend the role and responsibilities of the Duma, and demanding reforms the Tsar was not prepared to make. 'I created the Duma, not to be directed by it, but to be advised,'[4] he informed his Minister of War.

Finding the Duma threatened to undermine his powers, Nicholas suspended it after just two months. The second sitting lasted from February to June the following year, with Social Democratic Party members prepared to stand this time. But even their limited presence undermined the Tsar's authority, and again he found reason to suspend the Duma, arresting Social Democrat members for a suspected revolutionary plot uncovered by the *Okhrana* or state police.

By 1906 Piotr Arkadevich Stolypin had replaced the more liberal Witte. Stolypin, who previously had been involved in land reform, at first took the opportunity to alter the electoral system in favour of the country's landowners, and the next Duma (1907-12) saw a more moderate approach to government. With reforms in land ownership, education, local government and the army, Russia entered a period of relative stability and economic growth. But Stolypin was also aware that revolution remained a possibility and he took steps to improve employment in the cities, and to create a loan facility for limited land-ownership by peasants. This, however, made him unpopular with members of the Duma who thought his reforms were weighted in favour of the liberals. Even the Tsar finally turned against him, in part down to the influence of Father Grigory Rasputin. When Stolypin was assasinated in 1911, gunned down in his box at the theatre by a terrorist, some at court were less than sympathetic.

In 1912 the Duma came to the end of its five-year term and was reconstituted once again, leading to a few years of economic growth and increased national revenues.

In the last few years leading up to the First World War, Russia gravitated towards France and Britain as political allies, unable to agree with Germany over Turkish territories and shifting alliances in the Balkans. When Austria declared war on Serbia after the assassination of Archduke Ferdinand in June 1914, Russia was reluctantly brought into the conflict as an ally of Serbia. Soon countries within Europe were mobilising their forces in preparation for war.

The Duma was suspended temporarily in 1914, but by 1914-15 the military demands of the conflict were adding to Nicholas's problems. As the situation on the Eastern Front deteriorated, the clamour for a recall grew. Russia had not been ready to fight a war on such a large scale and as efforts faltered after initial gains, the Tsar sacked a succession of experienced ministers as scapegoats, including his Minister of War and Minister of the Interior. In August 1915 Nicholas gave in to demands to recall the Duma, hoping to strengthen his government and delegate some of the burden of responsibility. Instead, he found his government had become an increasingly vocal outlet for growing liberal frustration.

From the outset of the war, Russia had been in the grip of a fuel shortage, with Petrograd becoming increasingly dependent on coal from the south of the country as British and other European supplies were inevitably closed down by enemy action. Slowly over the next two years, food shortages added to wartime deprivation. As transport difficulties increased, localised shortages grew, and the inflationary financing of the war effort pushed prices ahead of wages. Towards the end of 1916, when the Tsar returned home from the Front for Christmas, Russian cities were reaching breaking point and it was estimated that Petrograd and Moscow were receiving only one-third of food requirements. Historian Richard Pipes noted that fuel shortages led to other difficulties: 'Petrograd could obtain only half of the fuel it needed, which meant that even when bakeries got flour they could not bake.'[5]

Nicholas's prolonged absence at the Front as Commander-in-Chief, coinciding with the end of the Duma's latest sitting, meant that he was now making ineffectual political and military decisions from Military Headquarters, far removed from Petrograd. To make matters worse, other individuals within court circles were beginning

to establish a degree of control. Such influences arrived in all shapes and sizes, from the Tsarina Alexandra and other Romanov relations, to those jockeying for political power within the government. In the midst of this growing uncertainty the enigmatic *staretz* or holy man from Tobolsk, Grigory Efimovich Rasputin, had been allowed to take centre stage.

Rasputin had been mentioned at court as early as 1905, but first came to the attention of the Tsarina in 1907. When her young son Tsarevich Alexei suffered a serious attack of haemophilia, Rasputin demonstrated that he could, with prayer or reassurance or even simple non-intervention, control the bleeding. The symptoms, including small haemorrhages, bruisings and swellings under the skin, had been detected soon after the Tsarevich's birth, and from that moment his parents lived in fear for his life. On one occasion, when Alexei was so ill that prayers were being said for him throughout Russia, Rasputin dispelled the Tsarina's fears by simply predicting the boy's recovery. Signs of improvement appeared the next day. As a result, Alexandra would hear nothing said against Father Grigory, and gradually she sought his advice on other things, including matters of state.

By 1916, however, rumours concerning the holy man's more disreputable activities outside the court were circulating wildly, and some members of Russia's élite were beginning to have serious concerns about Rasputin's hold over the Imperial family.

As the news from the war deteriorated and discontent gathered pace, Rasputin's influence on public affairs through Alexandra became increasingly apparent. The court felt itself to be at the mercy of a disreputable holy man who was suggesting capricious ministerial appointments to the Tsarina, who in turn persuaded her preoccupied husband to endorse them. An impassioned plea was made in the Duma by Vladimir Purishkevich, a well-known monarchist, who voiced 'the thoughts of the Russian masses' facing the prospect of government ministers being manipulated 'like marionettes' by Rasputin and the Tsarina.[6]

In late September 1916, Stopford had just returned from a trip to England with Foreign Office bags in his possession. In October he set off for Paris, on his way once again to Britain. When he arrived back in Petrograd, the city was covered in a blanket of deep snow and the Neva had frozen over.

By December 1916 Rasputin's ominous presence within the court was still the subject of lurid gossip and Stopford, through his network of Romanovs, was left in no doubt about their anger with the Tsarina. On the evening of 19 December Stopford bumped into Dmitri Pavlovich on leave from the Front, taking supper in a restaurant. Dmitri took Stopford aside and confided to him, rather mysteriously, 'the steps he thought must be taken to arrest the continued reactionary policy of the Empress, into which she was dragging the Emperor; and how imperative was the removal of evil counsellors'.[7]

The next day Stopford spent time with Dmitri at his palace apartment, returning for supper around midnight. Two days later he wrote a letter, hinting at possible future events:

> Strange things are happening here. ... I have been warned of a drama which may soon happen. But I dare not breathe a word. Even my frequent visits to Europe might count against me.[8]

Maria Pavlovna was also worried about the abuse of power at court. Her shocked reaction to her nephew's decision to take over the military command revealed her anxiety for the future, and she could see that Nicholas's absence had allowed others to take some degree of control. Maria now became increasingly critical among her closest friends, especially with regard to the Tsarina. It was true that she never had much time for Alexandra, despite the two women being of German birth. And it had not helped matters that Maria's son Kyril was barred from the succession by the Tsar when he married his cousin and divorcee Victoria Melita in 1904. (Victoria's first marriage had been to Ernst Ludwig of Hesse, Alexandra's brother.) Although Nicholas later changed his mind, the damage was done, creating lasting tension. Maria's loyalty to her nephew and niece had been tested to its limit.

* * *

Stopford spent Christmas Day 1916 [N.S.] at the British Embassy. During charades, he told Lord Buchanan that the Tsarina had left Petrograd to visit her husband at Military Headquarters.

Almost a week later, in the early morning of 30 December, Stopford was awakened in his hotel room by a member of staff bearing shocking news. Rasputin had been shot by Felix Yusupov.

Stopford telephoned the Embassy immediately and penned a note to Maria. That evening, at the French Theatre, Stopford took the opportunity to speak with Dmitri and Boris, but they did not appear to have any further information about the whereabouts of Rasputin or of what had happened to him.

The next day Stopford was no further forward. Over lunch at the Embassy with Lord Buchanan and General Hanbury-Williams, Stopford told them that he had written to London ten days ago, warning 'that the political situation [in Russia] would end in a tragic *denouement*'.[9] Surely this was confirmation.

While they were talking, a copy of the official Police Report was brought in. It contained an account of the arrivals, departures and police calls at the Yusupov Palace on the 29th of December. Out of the formal and pedantic prose, some interesting facts emerge. First, witnesses had confirmed that a body had been loaded into a car before being driven off from the palace. Second, Rasputin had indeed been killed in the Yusupov Palace. And third, Felix Yusupov himself had told the police that a report should be drawn up on the killing of Rasputin. Police officials had even been shown the spot in the palace where the body had been lying. But as police searched the islands of the Neva for a sighting of Rasputin, Yusupov refused to say anything more on the subject.

Stopford called in at the Vladimir Palace to tell Maria Pavlovna about the Police Report, only to find out that Dmitri Pavlovich had been placed under house arrest. Stopford then returned swiftly to the Embassy to get permission from Buchanan to show the Report to Maria, which was duly granted.

Later that day Maria spoke with Dmitri on the telephone. He admitted that he *had* been at the Yusupov Palace on the 29th [N.S.], but said that he had left at four in the afternoon. He fiercely denied all knowledge of the 'Rasputin affair'.[10] Although willing to submit to house arrest for form's sake, Dmitri let it slip that it was the Tsarina who had given the order for his detention. Maria was beside herself with anger. Even the Tsar had no constitutional power of arrest over a member of the Romanov family.

Felix Yusupov, meanwhile, was nowhere to be found, although a visitor to the Embassy said that she had recently seen both Yusupov and Dmitri at the Anglo-Russian Hospital. Yusupov was apparently having a fish-bone removed from his throat. To all who called in at the Yusupov Palace, however, it was claimed that Felix had left Petrograd for the Crimea.

* * *

In the immediate aftermath of Rasputin's death, Prince Felix Yusupov and Grand Duke Dmitri Pavlovich were sent away from the capital – Dmitri to Persia and Yusupov to his Rakitnoïe estate near Kursk. Dmitri's family was livid and prepared a petition to Nicholas to rescind the unlawful arrest – a snippet Stopford picked up at Maria's dinner-table. The petition, signed by Maria and her family, and Dmitri's father Pavel Alexandrovich, among others, was sent to the Tsar within the week. Pleading for clemency on the grounds of Dmitri's youth and state of health, they asked permission for him to retire to one of his own estates.

A swift and frosty answer was received from Nicholas: 'No-body has the right to kill on his own private judgment. … I am astonished that you should even have applied to me.'[11]

While London was a few days into its New Year, Stopford in Petrograd was faced with preparations for the Russian Christmas, running on the Old Style calendar. The extreme cold weather seemed to be causing him problems as the thermometer plummeted to between 20 and 36 degrees below zero. In a letter dated 2 January he complained to Lady Gladys that he was badly affected by 'awful rheumatism',[12] although it did not prevent him from keeping up with the latest whisper on the Rasputin case.

On Russian Christmas Eve Stopford joined other guests at the Vladimir Palace for Maria Pavlovna's celebrations. After dinner they moved into the ballroom where she took him aside to tell him that Dmitri had been deported to Persia at two that very morning, having been given only five hours' notice,[13] and the Tsar was still refusing to see Dmitri's father. Yusupov, meanwhile, had been sent from detention in Dmitri's palace to Rakitnoïe. Neither had been permitted to communicate with anyone, and no food had been provided for their respective journeys.

*   *   *

It was to be another six months before Felix Yusupov was able to tell Stopford his version of what happened on that terrible night in the Yusupov Palace. Felix, it appeared, had been at the very 'storm-centre'[14] of the murder, and in a letter to Lady Gladys Stopford was told her, in rather grand terms, 'The True and Authentic Story … as recounted to me on June 6, 1917, at Yalta by the Perpetrator'.[15]

Yusupov, it appeared, had wanted Rasputin removed from his position of influence at court, and he cultivated a friendship, intending to invite Rasputin to his palace without raising suspicion.

On the afternoon of Friday 29 December [N.S], Rasputin arrived as expected and Yusupov led him down a small staircase into a basement dining-room. Father Grigory was in a very talkative mood and the conversation turned to matters of state, with Rasputin revealing, among other indiscretions, that the Tsarina intended to make herself Regent on the 10th of January. Yusupov offered his guest some cakes and wine, deliberately laced with poison.

Meanwhile, in an upstairs sitting-room, Dmitri Pavlovich and a member of the Duma, Vladimir Purishkevich, were present. [According to the Police Report,[16] two members of the *demi-monde*, were also with them, although this was never admitted to.]

As time passed, the poison was obviously not having the desired effect. Rasputin was drowsy, but very much alive. With events taking this unexpected turn, Yusupov left his guest and went upstairs to borrow Purishkevich's revolver. With the gun hidden behind his back, he approached the semi-conscious man cautiously and shot him 'through the left side, below the ribs'.[17] Rasputin fell backwards onto a polar bear skin rug and lay still.

Yusupov ran upstairs to find Dmitri and Purishkevich. [The two ladies had been thrown out of the palace by this point.[18]] He then returned downstairs to check on the body. Bending over Rasputin, Yusupov was 'horrified to find the eyes were not only wide open, but gleaming with tiger-like fury'.[19] Struggling to his feet, Rasputin's hands grabbed Yusupov around the throat and shoulders, ripping off his epaulettes. He then lurched up the staircase and out of a side door into a forecourt next to the palace. Here, according to Yusupov, Rasputin collapsed into the snow.

Yusupov found Purishkevich upstairs and shouted at him to come out to the forecourt. There Purishkevich fired four times at Rasputin. Two bullets found their mark – one through the back of the head, the other point-blank through the forehead. The 'lifeless body'[20] was then dragged back inside the palace until a motor-car arrived. Once loaded up, the car was driven off to Krestovsky Island where the body was 'thrown into a hole in the ice of the Little Neva'.[21]

Stopford's account of the murder of Rasputin, as related to him by Felix Yusupov, leaves several questions hanging in the air. How exactly was Rasputin killed – by poisoning, a bullet, or drowning? And given the number of bullets fired, who actually killed him?

In his 1953 autobiography *Lost Splendour*,[22] Yusupov provided more details of the affair, including the presence of two other men – Dr Lazovert (there to administer the poison) and a Captain Ivan Sukhotin. An inquest held at the time of the murder, however, determined that the fatal shot was the one fired in the dining-room,[23] which would, in terms of that inquest, point to Felix Yusupov.

Over seventy years after the event, the demise of the Soviet regime opened up the State Archives in Moscow. Contemporary statements were unearthed from St Petersburg and Moscow, and a copy of the official investigation into the murder came up for sale at Sotheby's in London. It was now possible to throw new light on certain aspects of what actually happened, raising doubts against Felix Yusupov's version of events.

Edvard Radzinsky, the Russian playwright and historian, was the first to bring the new evidence together.[24] According to Radzinsky, when the conspirators shared their initial thoughts on the matter, Yusupov's wife Irina was sunning herself in the Crimea. Not only did Felix send her confidential news of the plot ('I'm terribly busy working on a plan to eliminate Rasputin'), but he even tried to involve her in his plans, pleading with her to return to the capital. His intention was to lure Rasputin to the Yusupov Palace with the promise of meeting Irina. As she had a reputation as a great beauty, her presence was sure to whet his well-known lascivious appetite. Irina did not get involved, however, and stayed on in the south.[25]

Radzinsky is convinced that other temptations were set in place for the night in question. Yusupov had already made a great effort to befriend Rasputin so that an invitation to his palace would not seem out of the ordinary. He was tempted there that day to meet with friends of Yusupov, including two women who were not of the *demi-monde*, but who were the ballerina Vera Karalli, a friend of Dmitri Pavlovich, and Marianna Derfelden, the daughter of Dmitri's stepmother Olga Pistolkors. Radzinsky is also convinced that the long preamble about poisoned cakes and wine was an embellishment by Yusupov. He believes that Rasputin refused the refreshment on arrival, and Yusupov left in a panic to ask his friends upstairs what to do. Felix returned to the basement with a revolver and shot Rasputin, leaving him for dead on the floor, and then went upstairs again. But when they all went down to the lower floor, Rasputin suddenly stirred and, after a terrible struggle, escaped outside. Yusupov, an amateur shot, had only wounded Rasputin, leaving him unconscious but not dead.

Radzinsky also throws cold water on the notion, maintained by Yusupov, that it was Vladimir Purishkevich who fired the final shot at Rasputin as he was trying to escape outside. Radzinsky is convinced that a few initial wild shots were fired, probably by Purishkevich, but there were two final shots, one in the back and a precision shot to the head. This begs the question – who was the *accurate* marksman? Radzinsky believes that it was 'Grand Duke Dmitri Pavlovich above all. A brilliant Guards officer, athlete and one-time participant in the Olympic Games',[26] as he certainly had the ability.

But what about the motive? Like many at court, Dmitri was angry that Rasputin was so close to the Tsarina and the Imperial family. He was also aware that, outwith court, the holy man's lewd behaviour and loose talk was bringing the family's name into disrepute. Having lived with Nicholas and Alexandra at some point after his father's morganatic marriage, the gossip about Rasputin and the Tsarina must have been hurtful to him. Dmitri had also been briefly engaged to Nicholas's daughter Olga before Rasputin had somehow contrived to ruin the relationship, so he certainly had enough motive to pull the trigger. Radzinsky believes that given all of the above, and the fact that Dmitri was in the Yusupov Palace on the night of the murder, and was armed with a revolver, it can be concluded that

> ... if anyone had personal reasons to do the peasant in, Dmitri did. It was Rasputin who had wrecked his betrothal; it was Rasputin who had told the scurrilous tales about him and his fiancée; it was Rasputin who had disgraced the Royal family in which Dmitri had been raised; and it was Rasputin who had caused the schism in the great Romanov family. ...[27]

Radzinsky adds that the Tsar's younger sister Olga had also reached the same conclusion. When Rasputin's death became common knowledge, she wrote in her diary: 'We have learned that Father [Grigory] has definitely been killed; it must have been by Dmitri.'[28] Dmitri's own sister Maria likewise suspected that her brother was involved, although he never confessed to her outright.[29]

In recent years there has been another investigation into Rasputin's murder by former Metropolitan Police Commander Richard Cullen and the historian Andrew Cook, who believe that a member of Britain's Secret Intelligence Service is to blame for the crime. Basing this theory on forensic evidence in Russia, and on intelligence files and testimony of relatives of SIS members, they conclude the bullet that killed Rasputin was fired by a man known as Lieutenant Oswald Rayner, a British naval officer and spy. Rayner knew Yusupov from his days at Oxford and was based at the British Intelligence Mission in Petrograd at the time.

In 2004/05 the forensic expert Derrick Pounder concluded that the fatal bullet came from a different gun to the one that inflicted the other wounds, and this was supported by the firearms department of the Imperial War Museum. The forensic evidence suggested that a lead unjacketed bullet, like those used in Webley revolvers issued to officers in Britain's SIS, may have been used.

As it was thought that Rasputin was against the war and had been trying to persuade the Tsarina to negotiate peace with Germany, Britain may have had a vested interest in having Rasputin removed from his position of influence. If Russia had withdrawn from the Eastern Front, Germany would have been in a better position to remobilise its Eastern forces against the Allies in the west.[30]

* * *

Whatever the truth about Rasputin's demise, the fears for the imminent collapse of the Tsarist regime remained. Russia was in a state of political and social turmoil, and following the murder of Rasputin events were about to take a turn for the worse.

In the first few months of 1917 one-day strikes were beginning to spread as factories ran out of fuel and workers demanded days off to search for food. The capital was also in the grip of one of its coldest seasons for years. Petrograd's winter was guaranteed to be excessively cold, but 1917 was worst than most, averaging 12°C below zero in the first three months, compared to +4.4°C the previous year. In Moscow it sank even lower to almost 17°C below. Fuel shortages soon led to factory closures, forcing workers onto the streets. The anticipated re-opening of the Duma on 28 February, with its inevitable denunciations of government policies, prompted the authorities to curb workers' unrest by taking the leaders of the

Petrograd Soviet into custody. But when rumours of food-rationing began to spread, further demonstrations were inevitable.

In the aftermath of Rasputin's murder, Stopford went out to the Feodorovski cathedral to observe the Imperial family. He could see recent events had affected them very badly. Nicholas was 'drawn and white, … [and] looked straight before him all the time', while Alexandra appeared flushed and very ill at ease.[31]

The following day, on the stairs of the British Embassy, Stopford bumped into George Buchanan who had just returned from an audience with the Tsar.[32] Buchanan had taken the opportunity to be frank with Nicholas about the current crisis and the extent of the Tsarina's unpopularity, even suggesting possible means of regaining the people's confidence. Nicholas thanked him politely, but Buchanan was aware that yet another unsuitable individual had just been nominated for a ministerial position and the choice was 'as bad as it could be'.[33] Nicholas, it seemed, was incapable of change.

When Stopford visited the Feodorovsky cathedral a few weeks later, he noticed it 'was overrun with secret police'.[34] Rumours of discontent in the Guards regiments were now circulating, and some of the grand dukes, including Andrei and Kyril Vladimirovich, who were implicated in a rumoured plot to overthrow Nicholas, were relocated outside Petrograd in an effort to weaken their opposition to the Tsar.

The news, although disconcerting, did not appear to curtail Stopford's round of social engagements, but the extreme cold, food shortages and trouble on the streets were taking their toll.

As ministers of the Duma wrestled with acute shortages and escalating civil unrest, liberal and socialist factions were beginning to work in tandem, intent on taking charge of central government. They were no longer prepared to work with the ministers who had been foisted upon them by Rasputin and the Tsarina, and members who were sympathetic to change, such as the moderate social revolutionary Alexander Kerensky, began to rise to the fore.

At the beginning of March [February O.S.], workers at a Petrograd factory made demands for increased wages and all the factory's employees were locked out. A strike committee was set up, and unrest escalated over the city. With no work and little food, demonstrations in the street became more desperate.

Maria Pavlovna now announced that she was planning to leave Petrograd, and on 4 March she set out for Kislovodsk in the Caucasus to visit Andrei, who had been dispatched there to avert a *coup* against the Tsar. Stopford came to Nicolaiski Station to see her off.

At the French Embassy on 7 March, Stopford heard of 'disturbances in the streets … and some tram-car windows smashed'.[35] A few days later he came across a peaceful demonstration of people singing the 'Marseillaise' and joined in, waiting to see if anything would happen. Cossacks stood among them, but they were quite restrained, chatting amiably to children standing nearby.

On 10 March, drawn to his hotel window at the sound of shouting, Stopford saw Cossacks clearing people off the street below him. Later, while dressing for a concert, he heard machine-gun fire. From the window he saw a crowd on the Nevsky Prospect fleeing for cover through a bottleneck of motor-cars and sledges.

> The poorer-looking people crouched against the walls; many others, principally men, lay flat in the snow. Lots of children were trampled on and people knocked down by the sledges or by the rush of the crowd.[36]

Stopford was incensed. 'I saw red. I put on a jacket without tie or collar or greatcoat, rushed to my third-floor lift. ... I thought, if I could rally the people, we could capture the guns.'[37] But the lift was full and the entrance hall crowded with people. By the time he forced his way outside, the guns had stopped and the street was clear.

Stopford returned to his room to finish dressing and set off through the empty streets to his concert, but it had been cancelled.

Back at the hotel Stopford spotted three machine-guns from the vantage point of an upper window. They were in the hands of the state police and strategically placed to cover the street. A hotel maid told him that a woman and three men had already been shot.

These clashes between strikers, police and military personnel were more serious than Stopford realised. Scores of people had been killed that day, while mobs had attacked jails and police stations, freeing political prisoners. The Tsar was away at the Front again, and had effectively cut himself off from the capital. Being told by the current Prime Minister Nikolai Golitsyn of the escalating crisis and the powerlessness of the Duma to act, the Tsar chose to suspend the parliament and gave orders to quell any disturbances. But his insistence on a curfew only led to further clashes in the streets, with terrible loss of life.

It was becoming very dangerous to get around Petrograd, yet Stopford was determined to keep up his usual round of visits to the embassies, ministries and restaurants where he might run into people with news. Cossacks were now patrolling the main thoroughfares, and the trams had been stopped. With no public transport and few sledges, Stopford walked everywhere, but he kept himself close to the walls, alert to the next disturbance.

On 11 March Stopford lunched at Donan's where he met Dolly Radziwill, Countess Kreutz, Prince Kudachev and Prince Boris Golitzin. The Countess invited him to a ballet at the Mariinsky

Theatre that evening. Later, as he returned to his hotel, Stopford passed the barracks of the Pavlovski Guards regiment and noticed 'much ferment among the soldiers at the gates and a great deal of very animated conversation'.[38] Soldiers returning to barracks were reluctant to continue intervening in strikes on behalf of the state.

That same day the increasingly detested police were given permission to wear the Pavlovski regiment's uniform by the colonel in charge. On hearing this, the troops in the barracks turned on their colonel and killed him,[39] setting in motion the first rumblings of mutiny within the Guards regiments of Petrograd.

In the evening Stopford and a friend Guy Colebrooke dined at l'Ours before leaving for the Mariinsky on foot. Finding the place deserted,[40] Countess Kreutz gave them a lift to a dance at the Radziwills. The great and the good of Petrograd had been looking forward to this event for weeks, and they were determined not to miss a party. But although the Radziwills had made an admirable attempt at grand hospitality, the conversation was dominated by tales of gunfire, near misses, and what might happen next.

Stopford ran into Boris Vladimirovich at the dance, but Boris had little news to tell him of his family. Later, Stopford found himself embroiled in a heated argument with Prince Golitzin over the actions of the police. Golitzin accused Stopford of over-reacting, which made Stopford very angry. 'It's damned hard lines asking for bread and only getting a bullet!'[41] But with few shortages at Dolly's that night, it was almost four in the morning before his hosts dropped him back at his hotel. Stopford watched as searchlights randomly swept across the Nevsky, radiating from the Admiralty Tower. But even this late, the occasional bullet could be heard.[42]

The 11th of March had also seen the Volinsky Guards regiment decide to join the fight on the side of the people against the Tsar; and as mutiny spread quickly from barracks to barracks, government control in the capital was effectively lost.

The following day Stopford encountered desultory gunfire as he made his way from a lunch appointment and on to the Embassy. Word had come through that the Olives, who lived opposite the Tauride Palace, were cut off by fighting and no one should attempt to get through. Stopford was intrigued:

> That immediately excited me to go, so I started off along the French Quay. I had just got to the Liteiny, and was in the act of crossing the street, when machine-guns began to fire, so I lay down in the snow and a fat woman of the people lay across my legs till the machine-guns had finished firing.[43]

With great difficulty he extricated himself from the lady, and set off towards the Olives' residence. Soon he encountered threatening crowds in the streets. Having witnessed a young officer, a mere boy, killed because he would not surrender his sword, Stopford turned down into the side streets to avoid trouble. But the main streets were now being swept continuously by machine-gun fire and Stopford lost his way. Asking a non-commissioned officer if he was heading in the right direction for the Potemkinskaya, near the Olives, the soldier indicated 'in purest English', that it was all a hell of a mess![44] The soldier, whose mother was English, was more than happy to escort Stopford safely to the Olives.

On the way the two men stopped at the Tauride Palace to watch the soldiers arrive to swear allegiance to the new authorities. But inside the palace, the members of the Duma were not sure of their own situation. Kerensky was keen to welcome the troops, but others refused to be so closely identified with revolutionary actions. Eventually an announcement was made that a provisional government had taken over from the Tsar and his ministers.

On 13 March Stopford was walking around the city to keep an eye on the state of key buildings, and residences belonging to absent friends. Although the Vladimir Palace remained unscathed, he heard that the Hôtel Astoria had been stormed by a group of demonstrators reacting angrily to being fired upon by a sniper from an upper floor. The hotel was badly damaged and several officers killed. Stopford had also been told that General Freedericksz' house across the city had been 'looted and set on fire by the mob. ... It was completely burnt out, only the outside walls remaining.'[45]

The danger continued to escalate. Given a lift by an Embassy colleague Commander Locker-Lampson, the car was shot through after Stopford got out of it.[46] He was also subjected to a humiliating search of his hotel room in the middle of the night by newly appointed military police searching for hidden weapons.

Political pressure was now reaching crisis point in Petrograd. When the hopelessness of the situation was conveyed to the Tsar at Moghilev, he immediately set out to return to the beleaguered capital. But the progress of the Imperial train was slow, as parts of the network had been captured by rebels causing endless diversions. After delays at Bologoe, the train was halted at Pskov on 14 March, the headquarters of Russia's Northern Army.

The Tsar, still unwilling to acknowledge the gravity of his situation, was faced with a constitutional crisis when his main strength, the army, had mutinied in the capital. While some in the Provisional Government wished to retain the monarchy as part of a new constitution, others were calling for its abolition. By the time the notoriously irresolute Nicholas had made a decision to offer concessions to the new authority, events had overtaken him, and the mood in the capital was now urging his abdication. When this was confirmed by his chief military commanders, Nicholas realised that he had no alternative. On 15 March 1917 [2 March O.S.], Tsar Nicholas II, the mighty 'Tsar of all the Russias', took the momentous decision to step down.

Representatives of the Duma asked Nicholas to sign the abdication document in favour of his thirteen-year-old son Alexei, but on consideration of the boy's precarious health Nicholas refused and passed the succession to his brother Grand Duke Mikhail Alexandrovich, although this was to prove unacceptable to the majority of the new government.

Nicholas Alexandrovich Romanov was escorted back to Petrograd, accompanied by two members of the Provisional Government and his top general, there to be deprived of all his powers and privileges. His wife and children had already been taken into custody at Tsarskoe Selo.

Stopford was trying to keep up with the fast-changing news, picking up snippets of information wherever he could. On 14 March he had joined George Buchanan and Lady Georgina at the Embassy to watch columns of troops 'crossing the Troitzka Bridge',[47] on their way to salute the new government at the Tauride Palace. Stopford had heard rumours that the Emperor's train had been halted at Bologoe, but knew nothing further. Buchanan had not been told anything official, although a press correspondent said that a delegation from the Provisional Government was on its way to Bologoe to inform the Tsar that his brother would be Regent in his place.

Stopford had also learned of the appointment of Prince Georgy Lvov as President of the new government. Lvov was a liberal monarchist who had been in charge of the All-Russian Union of Zemstvos at the beginning of the war. Alexander Kerensky was also brought into the government as Minister of Justice, as he had the support of the Petrograd Soviet behind him. Kerensky, a skilled lawyer, would prove to be the real power behind the new regime.

On the same day Kyril Vladimirovich was spotted at the Tauride Palace at the head of the Naval Guards, wearing a red bow on his uniform to pledge his support. A red flag was now flying high above his palace. Stopford was later scathing about Maria's son:

> The Kyrills are behaving tactlessly; he is attacked by all parties for his attempts to curry favour with the powers that be, at the expense of his family. *Kyrill Egalité!* A Radical newspaper said, 'Only rats leave a sinking ship'.[48]

The following day, 15 March, Stopford was at the Embassy when Lord Buchanan was called to the telephone. The Tsar had officially abdicated. His son Alexei would reign under the regency of Mikhail Alexandrovich. Russia was entering a new political era.

'... the *Revolution* began to-day!'[49] Stopford wrote.

AI-TODOR VILLA, *c.*1900

The family of Grand Duke Alexander (Sandro)
Mikhailovich and his wife Grand Duchess Xenia
Alexandrovna relax on the veranda of their villa at
Ai-Todor in the Crimea.

(© Hulton Archive/Getty Images)

CHAPTER NINE

Caucasus and Crimea

O N 16 March 1917 Mikhail Alexandrovich refused the accession, and as Nicholas had no intention of letting Alexei leave the care of his family, Russia became a republic. The Provisional Government emerged to take control, made up mostly of the liberal Cadet Party. But the powerful Soviet in Petrograd, including many Mensheviks, organised itself alongside the new government and rallied the workers and disaffected soldiers. The Soviet effectively took charge of the running of the capital, with local soviets set up to control the provinces.

The Provisional Government, under Prince Lvov, proceeded with caution, making judicial laws, abolishing the hated secret police and releasing political prisoners. The Soviet and the land-owning nobles, meanwhile, scrutinised their every move.

Albert Stopford watched from the sidelines as revolutionary fervour took hold of the country, and the fate of some of his closest friends hung in the balance. Although a semblance of normality seemed to be returning to Petrograd – he noticed that the old man running the music shop opposite his hotel had reopened for business – mob violence continued to rule the streets.

With looting and killing breaking out in indiscriminate pockets, Stopford was beginning to hear some dreadful accounts of terror and intimidation. General Stakelburg had been shot behind a lamppost on the Palace Quay and left naked in the road, while two priests had been mauled in the street.[1] These were not isolated incidents.

Members of the Tsarist court and government were now facing daily arrest. Countess Kleinmichel was taken into custody at the Duma, while Peter Bark at the Ministry of Finance was arrested along with his staff.[2] Stopford had also heard that Madame Stürmer, wife of the former Prime Minister, had tried to commit suicide when her husband was taken away on the orders of the new government.[2]

The symbol of Imperial rule – the double-headed eagle that embellished shops and institutions such as the Yacht Club – was already being removed, while the large crown on top of the Winter Palace was unceremoniously pulled down and a red flag hoisted. Soldiers were now digging graves in Petrograd's Champs de Mars for the victims of the riots.

Bread was at best soldiers' black bread, but it was often unavailable. When the hotel ran out of food, Stopford went round to the Embassy where they provided such rarities as sardines and jam. Sartorial habits were also changing dramatically. 'One dines in morning clothes – *en citoyen*,'[3] Stopford complained.

He was still finding that the best way to get around was to walk. With no trams the cab-drivers were becoming increasingly surly, overcharging or refusing fares. On 28 March, being ignored yet again at the hotel rank, Stopford finally snapped.[4] Speaking in French to a gathering crowd he told them that he had lived in Republican France for many years and that 'French cab-drivers were the servants of the public'.[5] When his outburst was translated, the cab-driver was dismissed off the rank.

But the greatest change encountered by Stopford was at the former Imperial Ballet. Having been present at the last performance before the abdication, with the grand dukes and families in their private boxes, Stopford noticed that their places had now been taken by strangers. The Imperial box itself, in the centre of the grand tier, remained empty until the beginning of the second act when two people walked in. When the 'Marseillaise' was played and encored, Stopford left. He was told afterwards that a man 'with long hair and a red tie' harangued the audience at the finale, and that audience members had joined the dancers on stage for another rendering of the 'Marseillaise'.[6]

With nothing to occupy his time on Sunday 18 March, Stopford took a train out to Tsarskoe Selo to find out what was happening in the area. Although there had been reports of skirmishes, all appeared to be quiet in the streets. Stopford watched a child on skis playing in the snow and noticed that an 'old friend who sweeps the leaves was not at his corner, but the mounted Cossacks were in their places and the usual policeman at the Park Gate'.[7]

Stopford went to check on Maria Pavlovna's palace, where he found 'everything in order, with sentries at the gates and the front door as before',[8] before calling on Pavel Alexandrovich who stayed nearby. Pavel had broken the news to Alexandra of Nicholas's abdication. She was, he said, 'completely broken down',[9] but the family was having to come to terms with the daily humiliation of being kept under close guard at the Alexander Palace.

The Tsar was brought back to Tsarskoe Selo on 24 March, and Stopford lost no time in making the acquaintance of the officer in charge of the family. Invited to dine with him, Stopford was able to pick up snippets of information over the dinner-table. The officer was being served the same food as the Romanovs, along with one bottle of wine a day. 'All the wine in the Imperial cellars is bottled in Russia,' Stopford noted. 'The bottles have the Imperial arms in the glass.'[10] He was also offered Hennessy brandy, sanctioned by Count Benckendorff who was still in charge of Nicholas's finances.

Stopford learned that the children had been ill with measles. Olga and Tatiana were beginning to recover, but Anastasia remained unwell. There was particular concern for Maria who had pneumonia and was breathing with the assistance of oxygen bags. Alexei, meanwhile, was up and about and taking lessons with his French tutor. It was said that Nicholas and Alexandra now dined in Alexei's playroom on the first floor, where tables were taken in already prepared. Alexandra, however, had little appetite and ate only chicken.[11]

Stopford also heard that negotiations had begun over Nicholas's money within Russia and abroad. 'In the course of conversation Count Benckendorff said the [Tsar] had no money abroad, and that the private fortune, including that of the children, amounted to little.'[12] His statement was in fact accurate and well informed. If taken seriously it might have saved a great deal of effort on the part of many later claimants to the supposed Romanov fortune in foreign banks – including the bogus Anastasia, Anna Anderson.

As this author discovered when conducting research for an earlier book at the State Archives of the Russian Federation in 1994,[13] the Imperial family's bank accounts were still intact and showed exactly what the family was worth in terms of their personal fortunes in 1917. The Tsar's own cash and investments were entirely in roubles and amounted to twelve million, about £1 million in 1917. This was eventually taken over, along with his palaces and estates, by the Provisional Government. He had no personal cash or investments abroad, since he had repatriated the residue in 1914. The children between them had about the same amount, twelve million roubles, in the Mendelssohn Bank in Berlin. As the war had prevented its repatriation, it was eventually ravaged by hyper-inflation in Germany in the early 1920s. By the time the cash and investments came to be claimed by their aunt Xenia Alexandrovna in 1933, the value was negligible.

* * *

On 30 March Stopford was shocked to read in the Russian morning papers that Grand Duchess Maria Pavlovna had been arrested at Kislovodsk in the Causasus. An anonymous, though well-informed, author of a book *The Fall of the Romanoffs*, originally published in 1918, mentions a letter sent by Maria to her son Boris through a trusted pro-monarchist general called Tchebykine, which been intercepted by the new government. In the letter she reinforced her view that

... the hopes of the Romanovs centred henceforth on the Grand Duke Nicholas [Nicholaevich] and that it would be wise, if he became the Commander in Chief, to predispose the army in favour of his ascending the throne later.[14]

The Soviets did not want Nicholas Nicholaevich back in charge of the army, as he was an experienced general and the people wanted an end to Russia's participation in the war. Nicolaevich was advised to head south to his family's estates in the Crimea. Boris, according to Stopford's information, had now been arrested.

Stopford had been contemplating a journey to the Caucasus since saying farewell to Maria at the railway station at the beginning of March. On 11 April he set off, telling no one of his plans, not even George Buchanan.

> Even if I don't see her she will know that I have made the effort. It's a long journey – three nights in the train; and I fear there is complete anarchy on the railways, the soldiers insisting on going first class without paying. But ... after all her kindness to me, it is the least I can do.[15]

The journey took four long nights and there was little chance of sleep with the antics of rowdy army deserters in the corridor. The train finally pulled into Kislovodsk at three in the morning and Stopford, having no hotel reservation, wandered towards a nearby church to watch the blessing of the peasants' Easter food, 'with day-light just glimmering and the bells ringing wildly in beautiful spring weather'.[16]

When he arrived at Maria's villa later that day, he was not sure whether he would be allowed to see her. Fortunately she had been granted permission by her captors to receive guests on Easter Day.

Maria had been more or less confined to the house under guard and Stopford read in the Petrograd newspapers that she had suffered from heart trouble after the shock of her arrest:

> ... the 'Red' Town Committee – which like all the provincial ones, is most virulent – came into her bedroom at 2.30 a.m. to read the *mandat d'arrêt*; and afterwards she had fainting fits and was unconscious for hours.[17]

Maria told Stopford, rather dramatically, that she could think of nothing else but the 'Ballad of Reading Gaol',[18] although she admitted that her treatment by the local authorities depended on the sympathy or otherwise of the officers who appeared at the villa from time to time. With the lease of her property at Kislovodsk set to expire, Maria intended to go to the Crimea where she had been offered a house. Stopford pointed out that there were more than enough Romanovs there already, as many had been ordered to go to their villas in the south, and suggested leaving Russia altogether for Finland. But when Maria eventually requested permission to attend a sanatorium in Finland, her application was refused by the government and she moved in with her son Andrei in Kislovodsk.

When Stopford returned to Petrograd, he was told that Boris was languishing under house arrest in his 'English cottage'[19] at Tsarskoe Selo and could not be contacted. Instead he went to see Pavel, and was pleased to hear that Dmitri remained safe in Persia. Pavel told him that Alexander Kerensky, the new Minister of Justice, under pressure from the increasingly influential Bolshevik faction in the Soviet, had recently decreed that no member of the Imperial family would be allowed to leave Russia until the end of the war.

The grip was also tightening on the finances of the Tsar and his relations as the Provisional Government took control of the source of their income from Crown lands, formerly controlled by the Tsar, and replaced it with a new, tightly controlled civil list. The Crown lands in particular had provided income known as *udely* or *appanage* from which the grand dukes and their families received annual income. Each grand duke, for example, had been entitled to 280,000 roubles a year (roughly £28,000 between 1914 and 1917, worth *c*.£1,206,000 today). This and other allowances had now been stopped at source, and for the present the families were simply left with their private estates and personal possessions. Nicholas had also been deprived of his regular allowances from the State Budget, and with his own income severely curbed, he was now expected to contribute to his family's day-to-day living from his private bank account.

*   *   *

By the end of April, Stopford was beginning to exhibit signs of stress. He had already endured rheumatism, extreme cold and hunger, and within a few days of his arduous journey from the Caucasus he succumbed to a fever and persistent cough. Stopford earlier confided to a colleague Sir George Arthur at the Embassy that he felt 'horribly tired' and 'very, very old',[20] but to add to his misery, he injured his face and wrist after being pushed off tram by a 'citizen soldier'.[21] Two members of the militia assisted him to the British Embassy where Lady Georgina bandaged his wrist.

Health alone might have persuaded Stopford to escape to a warmer climate, but a chance meeting with Serge Obolensky, and an offer to join him and his wife Catherine Yurievsky in the Crimea, kept the Englishman in Russia.

Stopford had already met up with Obolensky in Petrograd in 1915. Although struck by how splendid he looked in his officer's uniform, Stopford noticed how much the war had already changed him, 'as it has all of us'. He seemed 'a little older and more serious'.[22]

At the beginning of May, Stopford decided to travel to the Crimea to visit the Obolenskys who were staying at the Villa Mordvina in Yalta. To escape Petrograd was an enormous relief for Stopford, and even the journey from the station to the villa was utter bliss, as he was driven 'over the mountains and down the other side, through woods of wild pear, cherry and crab-apple in blossom'.[23]

Obolensky was shocked when he saw his friend, for the Bertie Stopford he knew had changed. The confident, affable Englishman was no longer so sure of himself.

> Every day [Stopford] took out a little green cloth and on that he laid out a deck of tarot cards. His fortune was coming out awfully badly for him. He said that something awful was going to happen every day – he was certain he was going to be killed by the *Bolsheviks*.[24]

Stopford had begun to rely on the cut of the cards since the previous year when he had predicted a terrible tragedy a week before it happened. Dining at the British Embassy in Petrograd on 30 May 1916, Stopford had teased a lady guest by offering to tell her fortune with his tarot cards. Her choice spelled out 'an unmarried man', 'a journey', 'an accident' and 'death'.[25]

Stopford was one of a handful of Embassy associates who had 'heard under seal of secrecy' that Lord Horatio Kitchener was due to travel to Petrograd on board the cruiser HMS *Hampshire*. In his company would be Mr Hugh O'Beirne, a former British Foreign Office minister who had been the Councillor of Embassy in Petrograd for nine years. O'Beirne was a very popular, and unmarried, colleague and was known personally to those around the table that evening. Stopford found himself troubled by the cards and what they might mean, but to the lady he said that according to the cards, a friend was making a journey to see her, but the identity of this friend had not been revealed.[26]

A week later, on the 5th of June, Stopford was at the Embassy playing bridge with visiting American bankers when he was called to the telephone to be told the dreadful news that Lord Kitchener and everyone on board the HMS *Hampshire* were lost at sea. The ship had been sunk west of the Orkney Islands by a German mine. Stopford recalled the message conveyed by the cards and the fate of Hugh O'Beirne among those lost on the ill-fated *Hampshire*. 'My knees gave way beneath me: I collapsed.'[27] The cards had spoken.

Yalta's pleasant climate and the opportunity for rest brought some measure of calm nonetheless, and Obolensky's wife Catherine encouraged Stopford to stay longer. There were a few friends in town he could visit, such as Princess Orlov and the Bariatinskys, and as he

slowly gained his strength Stopford used his time to pick up news of other Romanovs who had fled to their villas nearby.

He learned that the former Empress, Maria Feodorovna, was staying in Ai-Todor at the villa of her daughter Xenia and husband Alexander Mikhailovich (known as Sandro). Maria had been living in Kiev since 1915, and watched in horror from the sidelines as one crisis after another led to her son's abdication. When the Provisional Government ordered her to leave for the south, Maria agreed with great reluctance. She was desperate to stay as close as possible to Nicholas and her grandchildren as they faced life in captivity.

Stopford wrote a letter on 15 May detailing an incident that had happened to the Empress only a few days earlier.[28] At about two or three in the morning a group of Bolshevik sailors from Sebastopol had turned up at the villa at Ai-Todor, without authorisation, and ordered the Empress out of bed. As she sheltered behind a screen, mattresses were ripped apart and icons split open. The sailors removed letters and an old bible brought from her Danish homeland before her wedding. When they did not find her jewels, or any items of significant value, they moved on to Xenia's room. Forcing her husband out at gunpoint, they kept the Grand Duchess under close guard until they finished searching the property.

The sailors then went to the villa of Grand Duke Nicholas Nicholaevich, who was staying on his brother's estate at nearby Djulber. Again, they found little of value.

On 16 June another member of the exiled community, Princess Serge Dolgoruki, died unexpectedly from an accidental overdose of veronal. Stopford was invited to attend her funeral at a small chapel in the woods close to the sea. It was the first Russian funeral Stopford had witnessed, and he was particularly moved by the stream of villagers who placed flowers near the coffin, and the simple devotional act of kissing the Princess goodbye.

Finding themselves increasingly subject to the whims of local factions, the Romanovs knew they could never be safe in the current political climate. Compelled to register their whereabouts, although largely left to manage their own affairs, the former members of Russia's élite were effectively under house arrest. They now became more determined than ever to salvage whatever they could of their past way of life.

CHAPTER TEN

Plotting

ON 15 May 1917, a week after Stopford's arrival in Yalta, Felix Yusupov paid a visit. He had travelled with his family to their Koreitz estate in the Crimea, having already begun to gather together what he could of their scattered possessions. These were not inconsiderable. At the outbreak of the war Yusupov's father was one of the richest men in the world, his wealth probably outstripping that of the Tsar.[1] The family owned thirty-seven properties and estates throughout Russia and abroad, the main ones being the Yusupov Palace near the Moika Canal in Petrograd, Arkhangelskoïe outside Moscow, Rakitnoïe near Kursk, and two estates, Kokos and Koreiz, in the Crimea. It was said they owned so much land that Felix's father once gave his wife a mountain for her birthday.

But given the uncertainty of his family's current circumstances, Yusupov was faced with a dilemma, for he could only save possessions that could be easily transported without attracting unwanted attention.

At Yalta, Stopford was delighted to be back in the company of his friends, and they had much to talk about. With Felix exiled after the murder of Rasputin, and Bertie under fire in Petrograd, only Obolensky had seen active service, fighting on the German and Austrian Fronts with the Chevalier Guards. But having been badly affected by shell-shock and suspected tuberculosis, doctors in Petrograd sent him to Yalta for a period of convalescence.[2]

Life had changed dramatically for all three, and thoughts were now turning to the practicalities of retrieving personal belongings from hastily abandoned palaces and residences. The recent incursion of sailors into the bedroom of Maria Feodorovna at Ai-Todor had sent shockwaves through the Romanov community in their Crimean villas. No one was safe. Maria's younger daughter Olga, living with her husband Nikolai Kolikovsky in a separate house on the same estate, had hastily hidden her mother's jewels in cocoa tins around her home. Whenever a search was threatened, Olga and Nikolai would hastily tuck the tins into crevices over the edge of a cliff on the seashore. Olga said they sometimes marked a particular spot with the skull of a dog, but on one occasion, after the danger had passed, they found the skull had been disturbed.

> I still remember the cold drops of perspiration forming on my forehead as I watched my husband sticking his hand deep in every possible hole in the rock face. What a relief when he finally pulled a cocoa tin rattling with jewels out of one hole![3]

Yusupov told Stopford that he had already begun to smuggle some of his family's possessions out of Petrograd. After a previous trip he returned to the Crimea bearing two valuable paintings and a pocketful of jewels. The paintings were Rembrandts, cut from their frames in the Yusupov Palace. *The Man in the Large Hat* and *The Woman with the Fan* were among the finest portraits in the family collection. 'Unframed and rolled up, the paintings were easy to carry,' he explained, but his journey back to the Crimea had been a less than comfortable experience:

PRINCE SERGE OBOLENSKY, 1917

Serge Obolensky (1890-1978), painted in 1917 by the esteemed portrait artist Saveli Sorine. Obolensky remained a loyal friend to Albert Stopford over the years. A photograph of the painting was used in his book, *One Man in His Time*.

A crowd of soldiers who had demobilised themselves, but kept their arms, filled the train. There were as many piled on the roofs of the coaches as inside them. In fact one coach collapsed under their weight. As they were all more or less intoxicated, several fell off during the journey. The farther south we went, the more crowded the train became, chiefly owing to the civilians who were seeking shelter in the Crimea. Eight of us, including an old woman and two children, were huddled together in what was once a compartment of a sleeping car.[4]

Although not referred to in his diary, one may reasonably assume that Stopford discussed plans to rescue additional possessions and valuables with his Russian friends during his extended visit to the Crimea. He obviously felt a personal loyalty to them in their adversity and had been toying with similar thoughts since his last visit to Maria Pavlovna in Kislovodsk. Although he had been able to reassure the Grand Duchess that the Vladimir Palace in Petrograd was still intact, other palaces had not been so lucky.

I hear that all the palaces which were inherited by the Imperial family have been made national property – like the Winter Palace, the Tsarskoe Selo palaces, Peterhof and Oranienbaum; but palaces built or bought by the Imperial family will continue to belong to them.[5]

On 30 April 1917 Stopford wrote that Maria's palace at Tsarskoe Selo had been perequisitioned by the new government. The housekeeper had left the lights on by mistake during the night, prompting military police to overrun the building. The authorities took the opportunity to make an inventory of the palace,[6] as Maria's former position in the Tsarist court and her German origin continued to raise suspicion under the new regime.

In her safe was found a book which the Red newspapers allege is a German cipher – the fools! They have since had to admit it was the key to the working of the safe, which had only lately been put in and which, like everything else in Petrograd, was 'made in Germany'.[7]

It is known from Obolensky's autobiography *One Man in his Time*[8] that Stopford and Yusupov made several return journeys to Petrograd from Yalta with the sole intention of gathering easily portable valuables; sometimes working together, sometimes alone. It is also known that Yusupov made at least three visits on his own account and one, much later, on behalf of Maria Feodorovna. But the timing of these forays is more difficult to determine, as Yusupov and Stopford remained tight-lipped about their activities. Details in Stopford's diary are scant during May, showing a gap between the 5th and 15th, and then nothing until 31 May when he was supposedly relaxing in Yalta. This is perhaps the only significant clue as to timing.

At some point during his stay in the Crimea, Stopford seems to have made a personal decision to go into the Vladimir Palace to rescue Maria Pavlovna's jewels and money before the authorities took over the building. Travelling back by train to Petrograd at the end of June, he took a keen interest in the military presence within each railway compartment, thinking that such attention to detail would be of use to him on future journeys.

At important stations the door to each corridor was guarded by a sentry with fixed bayonet to prevent deserters or the unauthorised entry of soldiers:

> The man on guard at my carriage was leaning against the train, smoking, with his rifle held anyhow. I said in English, with an air of authority, 'You know you are on duty; why the hell don't you take the cigarette out of your mouth and hold yourself straight?' The inflexion of my voice and the atavism of obedience were enough: he instantly threw away his cigarette and stood to attention![9]

Stopford concluded that even a languid foreigner might wrong-foot an ill-trained recruit. Perhaps this would prove to be the best way to avoid suspicion if, on some future journey, he had something to hide.

Back in Petrograd at the beginning of July 1917, Stopford faced the latest twist in the dual-power co-existence between the liberal members of the Provisional Government, and the moderate socialists of the Petrograd Soviet (the *Mensheviks*) and the more extreme left-wing *Bolsheviks* led by Vladimir Ilyich Ulyanov, known as Lenin.

On 3 July Stopford noticed 'a state of general tension'[10] all over the city, with soldiers very much in evidence on the streets. But as he had made plans to catch up with friends after his prolonged absence in the Crimea, he ignored the military presence and set off for the British Embassy and Russian Foreign Office. Later he took a trip out to Tsarskoe Selo to see Boris, who was no longer under house arrest.

Felix and Irina Yusupov had also returned to Petrograd, clearly intent on removing more family possessions. Stopford spent the afternoon of 4 July with them at the Yusupov Palace, where he was shown the bear skin where Rasputin had fallen and told the entire sorry tale once again.

Only days later conditions in Petrograd were beginning to alarm Stopford. The fear in the streets had spilled over into violent demonstrations as armed soldiers and disaffected workers clashed with the authorities.

The Provisional Government was beginning to lose control of the city. After the February/March revolution the Petrograd Soviet had watched its every move with suspicion, and in two crucial matters it deemed that the government had failed the people. Russia was still involved in the war, and the peasant classes had still not received favourable land reform. When Paul Miliukov, the Minister for War, dared to suggest that Russian forces would be used in an offensive role, against the will of the Soviet, Prime Minister Lvov was forced to change Miliukov for Alexander Kerensky who was trusted by the workers as a Social Revolutionary member of the government. Kerensky immediately set about strengthening the armed forces, but his attempts were to be shortlived. Having encouraged his reinvigorated troops back into battle against the Germans and Austrians, he was shocked to find his army faced with relentless defeat.

Lenin, the enigmatic Bolshevik leader, was back in Petrograd after ten years of exile, desperate to stop his Party supporting the outcome of the February/March revolution, and the Soviet co-operating with the policies of the Provisional Government. For Lenin, the war in Europe was a capitalist war and would not solve Russia's problems. The revolution of the proletariat was yet to come.

The Bolsheviks immediately implemented their plans to gain power within the soviets and started distributing propaganda on the promise of 'Peace! Bread! Land!' They were soon in a position to exploit any unrest within the peasants and workers, and take advantage of growing mutiny among the troops at the Front.

Back in the cities the people now experienced the combined food shortages, rationing, job losses and rising prices. Such hopeless conditions would lead to the uprising of the 'July Days'.

＊　＊　＊

Stopford woke up in his hotel on the morning of 13 July to discover that the staff were on strike. He made his bed, cleaned the bath, swept his room, and did the same for the lady along his corridor who had terrible rheumatism. As he was expecting guests for lunch, he raided the abandoned kitchens of the hotel for whatever food he could find and carried it back to his room.

On the evening of 16 July Stopford went to the Yusupov Palace for supper and entertainment in celebration of Irina's birthday. But there was already trouble brewing on the streets and along the Nevsky Prospect Stopford saw armoured cars and motor-lorries revving menacingly up and down the main thoroughfare.

At the palace Stopford joined the guests, including Lady Muriel Paget, in the basement dining-room. As they listened to the music of guitarist Sacha Markarov, an armed regiment was gathering along the opposite side of the Moika. Stopford later heard that Cossacks had suddenly appeared and civilians and soldiers scattered into nearby houses and courtyards, many falling under hooves and gunfire.

News of the fierce disturbances was relayed by telephone to the palace, but guests could already hear the shooting and screaming outside. Lady Muriel asked Stopford to take her back to the Anglo-Russian Hospital, as a call had come through from the porter at the hospital to say that he had just seen two rider-less horses pass by and he was worried for her safety.

Stopford was happy to accompany Lady Muriel back to the hospital, but he had some rules. 'He was very amusing about rules and instructions as to behaviour during a revolution,' Lady Muriel later said, 'and assured me that if I obeyed him implicitly all would be well.'[11] She was to avoid open spaces and wide streets, keep well into the wall in side streets to avoid surging crowds, and lie on her face on the ground in the event of gunfire breaking out.

They left the palace down a side street and hired an *isvoschiki*, but the cab barely moved before a crowd carrying revolutionary banners blocked their way and 'an armoured car with guns pointing from it in every direction passed along amid cheers from the crowd'.[12] When Cossacks appeared, part of the crowd took fright and poured down the side street towards Stopford's cab. Lady Muriel scrambled out and hid against the walls of a house. The driver complained bitterly, but was pulled down by the mob. Stopford found himself tumbled out of the back.

> An old woman was hobbling along on two sticks, which were knocked out of her hands in the rush, and she fell on her knees. I picked her up, gave her her sticks, and propped her against the wall. I then called out to Lady Muriel, and fortunately she heard me. I told her to lie down near the wall, as there was no courtyard near to get into; but on second thoughts I hurried her down the street and we found one.[13]

Later, walking cautiously along the side of the Fontanka Canal towards the hospital, they were warned that streets around the Nevsky were still dangerous, but it seemed relatively calm. Many of the wounded had already been admitted to the hospital, and Stopford found out that the fighting had been between Bolshevik soldiers and Cossacks trading gunfire at the corner of Vladimir Prospect. When Stopford returned to his hotel at quarter past two in the morning, casualties were still lying bleeding on stretchers in the street.[14]

Sporadic shooting continued the next day as Stopford made his way around the streets. During lunch the familiar sound of machine-gun fire could be heard, bullets ricocheting off the roof opposite. Stopford stayed in the hotel that evening and made do with tea and jam. The hotel cooks were still on strike.

The next day, as he crossed the Champs de Mars on his way to the British Embassy, Stopford encountered soldiers sitting in the windows of the nearby Pavlovsky barracks, deliberately firing over people's heads. 'I was not going to turn back for them. I pulled myself together and walked across the Champs de Mars and entered the Embassy by the adjoining courtyard.'[15] Finding Lord Buchanan beside an upstairs window, the two men watched as soldiers advanced cautiously on their stomachs over the Troitzka Bridge.

With reports coming in of severe fighting breaking out near the Nicolai railway station, Stopford could see no end to the misery:

> We have had five days' hell. Tuesday was worse than any day in the [First] Revolution. ... You have no idea how tired it makes one; I sleep eight hours, only to wake up much more tired. There is nothing to eat, either; I am always hungry.[16]

Felix Yusupov's account of the same week was just as bleak:

> Trucks filled with troops drove through the city, shooting off machine guns; soldiers crouching on the running boards shot at any unfortunate pedestrians who had failed to take cover. The streets were strewn with the dead and wounded; the capital was in a state of panic.[17]

CHAPTER ELEVEN

Saving the Jewels

THE sense of panic that gripped Petrograd during the 'July Days' lasted almost a week before Kerensky's troops gradually extinguished the latest threat to the government's fragile co-existence with the Soviet. But Lenin's propaganda on 'Peace! Bread! Land!' had gained momentum with the workers and the threat of political violence did not diminish.

The government blamed the Bolsheviks for the latest uprising, although this was not the case, and accused its members of acting as spies for Germany by attempting to disrupt Russia's war effort. Lenin was forced into hiding, while Leon Trotsky, now a Bolshevik, gave himself up and hotly denied any association with Germany.

By 21 July Alexander Kerensky had replaced Prince Lvov as Prime Minister of the Provisional Government, but his known sympathy towards the Soviet did little to endear him to Russia's military leaders and land-owners who both wanted the power of the soviet destroyed.

Albert Stopford watched the political fall-out with growing concern. Time was rapidly running out to implement his plan to rescue Maria Pavlovna's jewels and money from the Vladimir Palace.

Stopford knew the palace well and had walked past it many times. He had also been a guest there at one of Maria's lavish receptions, or informally to share some private news or gossip, and he could imagine going into the palace through the three-arched portico facing the Neva, then walking into the hall and up the grand staircase to the magnificent ballroom or Red Salon. But locating Maria's jewels in the private quarters of the vast Vladimir Palace would not be so easy.

Success or failure depended on knowing exactly where Maria's jewels were hidden, and on finding the quickest route in and out of the palace without detection. With Maria and Boris eager to help, the task would be made a lot easier.

Stopford and Boris agreed that the main entrance to the palace on the side of the Embankment was far too exposed. Even if Stopford was able to avoid being spotted from that direction, he would remain

THE VLADIMIR PALACE,
ST PETERSBURG

The Vladimir Palace, residence of the Grand Duke
Vladimir Alexandrovich and the Grand Duchess
Maria Pavlovna until 1917.

(© Martin Anderson)

vulnerable as he made his way up the grand stairway and through the maze of reception and drawing-rooms.

In addition to the main Florentine portico entrance with its over-hanging balcony, there were two smaller doorways – one that led from a courtyard on the west side to the late Grand Duke Vladimir's private apartments, and a similar doorway on the east side where the kitchens were located.[1] At the back of the building there was also an entrance on the Millionaya.

But there was another possibility. Maria and Boris told Stopford of a secret passageway that led directly from an entrance at the side of the palace to Maria's Moorish-style boudoir on the first floor. A concealed door in the wall of her room led to several passage-ways.[2] (This entrance was sealed off in 1920 when the palace became the House of Scientists during the early years of the Soviet regime.)

Anyone entering Maria's boudoir would have immediate access to her study overlooking the Neva (the Pear Living-Room), her bed-room (now known as the Green Living-Room), and her dressing-room, wardrobe and bathroom. The jewels, according to Maria, were kept in a locked metal safe located near the dressing-room and wardrobe.

Serge Obolensky, in his book *One Man in his Time*, maintained that Boris Vladimirovich accompanied Stopford when he went into the palace:

> When the Grand Duchess Maria fled to the Caucasus at the begin-ning of the Revolution, she left cash and all her jewels in the safe in her palace in St Petersburg. She was getting short of cash. In disguise Grand Duke Boris and Bertie got into her palace on the Neva with the help of a caretaker who remained loyal. They made their way to the Grand Duchess's bedroom, to the secret safe she told them about, and took out all the jewels and the money.[3]

Despite Obolensky's account, it is more likely that Stopford went alone, although, in agreement with Obolensky's version of events, he did ensure beforehand that access would be possible during the night, with the help of the palace's caretaker.

Dressed as a workman, Stopford left his hotel and made his way to the palace. Checking he was not being watched, he got in through the entrance at the side of the palace and moved quickly through the secret passageway to Maria's boudoir with its suite of rooms. Find-ing the safe exactly where it had been described, he unlocked it to reveal the treasure hidden inside.

Stopford carefully dismantled the jewellery, folding the bits into old newspaper to protect them, and placed the packages gently into two shabby Gladstone bags.[4] Some of the tiaras, however, were kept intact. There was also money inside the safe, and that too was placed into the bags.

This was perhaps the easiest part of his mission. If Stopford had already assisted Yusupov with previous rescue missions over recent months, he would know the risk he was taking. But this time he was facing that risk alone. The streets were full of police and soldiers, and if confronted and searched it would be difficult to explain why he was carrying two bags full of precious jewels and a wad of money. He was running a very real risk of being arrested, even shot, for looting or theft. And as he could not implicate Maria or Boris in his actions, there was no one who could save him.

Relief at his success in removing the valuables was tempered by anxiety, and it was perhaps a less assured Stopford who retraced his steps down the passageway and out of the side door that night. Every creak in that vast empty palace, every burst of gun-fire from the streets outside, must have heightened his sense of fear.

Stopford now faced a number of dilemmas. First of all, since his hotel room had already been searched by military police, he could not hide the jewels there until he was ready to smuggle them out of Russia. Stopford did indicate on 29 January 1917 that he kept private papers, including his diary, in the Chancery at the British Embassy. Is it possible that the jewels were kept there as well?

Second, he would have to find a way to spirit the jewels out of the country without incurring suspicion. Should he use his privileged position at the British Embassy to smuggle the jewels out to London using the diplomatic bag? Or should he carry the Gladstone bags out in person during one of his trips back to Britain?

And third, Stopford now faced a difficult journey to Kislovodsk through countryside swarming with ill-disciplined soldiers in order to get the money to Maria as soon as possible.

On 27 July Stopford went out to Tsarskoe Selo to tell Boris that the contents of his mother's safe had now been removed from the Vladimir Palace. He also found out the latest news on Nicholas and his family, who were rumoured to be heading for Tobolsk in Siberia.

The next day Stopford started out on a journey he was unlikely to forget. As a fifty-seven year-old English gentleman wearing western clothes, Stopford must have cut a conspicuous figure among the crowds of soldiers on the train. But perhaps his bearing did serve to deter any unwelcome approach as he was left well alone. This was fortunate, as his boots were stuffed with thousands of roubles.

Stopford arrived at Kislovodsk in the early morning of Monday 30 July and was warmly welcomed by Maria Pavlovna who invited him to stay at Andrei's villa. That night they sat round the dining-table until midnight, mulling over the latest news from Petrograd and the plight of mutual friends before counting the money retrieved from Stopford's boots. He had already had it exchanged into revolutionary thousand rouble notes which Maria did not recognise.

Stopford stayed on for a few days to celebrate Maria's fête day of St Mary Magdalen. He found some tuberoses to give as a gift and they enjoyed lunch on her veranda with a number of other guests.

On 5 August 1917 Stopford took his leave of Maria Pavlovna, who asked him to pass on her regards to his King and Queen, and to assure them of her deepest affection. She added that she was very envious of people who live in a country where there are policemen.[5] It is not known whether Stopford ever had the opportunity to take this message to King George in person.

Back in Petrograd, Stopford called on Boris to tell him how his mother was faring. He then went to have lunch with General Sir Charles Barter and General Alfred Knox, the top British military commanders in Russia. Later that evening he could be found in the company of Lord Ilchester, a King's messenger, relaxing at a party in the Yusupov Palace. Stopford was quickly back into his routine again and picking up the latest information in the capital in his own inimitable style.

* * *

On 14 August 1917 the Imperial family began their journey under guard from Tsarskoe Selo to Tobolsk. As the political struggle for power within the factions of the government rumbled on, the fate of Nicholas and Alexandra and their five children hung in the balance. Alexander Kerensky finally took the decision to send them to Siberia – for their own safety, he stressed – prior to an official inquiry to clear them of treason.

While visiting Boris at Tsarskoe Selo, Stopford found out more about the Romanovs' unceremonious departure. In a letter to Lady Gladys de Grey he told her that the family had been unnecessarily delayed for a number of hours and that they did not leave until 5.35 in the morning. The Guards had saluted the Tsar as he, Alexandra and Alexei were driven to the station in one car, his four daughters in another. The heads of the girls had been shaved because of their recent bout of measles.

> The Emperor lit cigarettes incessantly, and threw them away. The Empress had tears in her eyes. The Grand Duke Alexei cried, poor little boy! ... The four Grand Duchesses showed no emotion.[6]

Boris said that the Tsar's brother Mikhail had endured a poignant last meeting with Nicholas, and at Boris's house Mikhail was 'so upset that he could not speak'.[7] Kerensky, however, had given his word that the family would be back by November.

The decision to transfer the Romanovs from Tsarskoe Selo to Tobolsk was indicative of a number of cross currents. The Provisional

91

Government, concerned at the possibility of a right-wing *coup* or counter-revolution, was also being kept constantly under pressure by the Bolsheviks. Tobolsk was far enough away to reduce any chance of them being rescued as it was not even on the railway system. But it must have occurred to Nicholas that any possibility of exile to the Crimea, or even abroad to relatives in Britain or other allied European state, was rapidly disappearing.

Following the quelling of the latest disturbances, Stopford was now finding life in Petrograd intolerable:

> … last night, coming away from the Yusupovs', there was a rifle-shot quite close to me. Nowadays a single shot can bring on a battle. One is almost more apprehensive of calm than of noise. … Want of bread brought on the Revolution and the same may bring on a counter-revolution. There is nothing to eat. …[8]

In the early hours of Saturday 11 August, Stopford had been walking down the Morskaya on his way back from a supper-party, when a sentry blocked his way. As Stopford moved to pass, the soldier rushed at him with a fixed bayonet pointed at his chest. By good fortune the conductor of the ensemble that had played at the party was passing in his carriage and jumped out to shout at the soldier, who lowered his bayonet. 'Better go to the Front and kill Germans than a peaceable ally!'[9] the conductor remonstrated. But Stopford knew at that moment that it was time for him to leave Petrograd. The risks were becoming far too great.

As his plans to return to London took shape, Stopford was determined to bring himself up to date with the latest news of the war by visiting the Military Headquarters at Moghilev.

> Monday, Aug. 20: Arrived Moghilev 1.40pm; Staff automobile to meet me. To Hôtel Bristol, where the Allied officers are lodged.[10]

Stopford was received at Military Headquarters as a familiar face. He was by this time known to many of the officers and staff, and privy to candid discussions and information.

After meeting with the Russian General-in-Command at the headquarters of the Russian Air Force, the head of the Allied Staff, Sir Charles Barter,[11] invited him to lunch with other Allied officers from France, Italy and Romania. Stopford was delighted that one of his table companions was a Russian called Mordveno, whom he met in Yalta when staying with the Obolenskys. After lunch Barter offered Stopford a cigar and told him many 'interesting things'[12] that were not divulged in his diary at that time.

Stopford returned to Petrograd in a special military coach attached to the Kiev express, guarded by a non-commissioned officer and two soldiers. A cousin of the King of Montenegro, George Popovich, shared his compartment. He was a friend of Kerensky's new Commander-in-Chief, General Lavr Kornilov.

What turned out to be Stopford's last weeks in Petrograd were more tiring and difficult than his experiences during the February/March Revolution and the 'July Days'.

> Some one says, 'The fear of Russia is worse than Russia,' and I am sure it is true. During the actual riots I thoroughly enjoy the street fighting, but I am worried to death while it threatens, and dead tired after it is over.[13]

In truth Stopford was a spent force, worn down by stress, travel and lack of food: 'I must rest. I am nearly as thin as when I was so ill; there is nothing to eat here – no butter for four days',[14] and little if any bread either. But there would be no respite, as another threat to the uneasy peace in the capital began to emerge.

While at Moghilev, Stopford had been alerted to the possibility of a potential *coup d'etat* by General Kornilov, and he was cautiously optimistic of its success.

> Have just seen a procession with Red Flag, so I suppose we are in for more riots – a great nuisance. The Government weakens daily, and at the appointed time Kornilov will come at the head of a regenerated army to save Petrograd. If he succeeds, then an Emperor in three months, I say![15]

General Lavr Kornilov, a soldier with an impressive war record and noted for his discipline, was appointed Commander-in-Chief of the Provisional Government's forces in July 1917. He believed that the war against Germany and her allies should continue and feared for the future of Russia under Soviet control. As part of his appointment, Kornilov demanded of Kerensky that army committees should not be subjected to political interference, and that railways and munitions factories should be placed under military control. Kerensky, caught between the Soviet and his own government, realised that his Commander-in-Chief could count on the support of other generals. When Kornilov resisted attempts by Kerensky to water down his demands, the situation deteriorated to the point where Kerensky moved to dismiss Kornilov. This raised expectations of a military response. As Kornilov began to assemble his troops outside Petrograd, officers within the city were notified by the General to be ready to break up the Soviet and hang the pro-German Bolsheviks.

Stopford's intelligence, gathered from various contacts, gave him reason to believe that Kornilov had gained the support of 600,000 Cossacks, cavalry, and the greater part of the South-Western Army. Since Kornilov had been greeted with great acclaim when he last came to the capital, Stopford was fully expecting him to march into Petrograd at the head of his Cossacks to take over power.

> Tuesday, Sept 11: My windows open all day, in order to hear the first signs of the Cossacks' arrival. As the afternoon advanced and I heard no firing, my heart sank … the *coup d'etat* had failed.[16]

The beleaguered Kerensky had been saved by workers and soldiers loyal to the Soviet who set up barricades to defend Petrograd. With them, standing shoulder to shoulder, were thousands of members of the new Red Army, workers who had been armed by the Bolsheviks.

With the railways sabotaged and lines of communication disrupted and distorted, Kornilov was destined never to reach Petrograd. Infiltrated by Bolshevik agents, his army succumbed to mutiny and swiftly dispersed.

Kornilov had not taken his opportunity and the last chance of a right-wing *coup* vanished with it. With Kerensky irrevocably weakened and the Bolsheviks riding a wave of popularity, Russia was now weeks away from Lenin's final triumph.

The impact on Stopford was marked:

> These last few days have seemed like a lifetime. Yesterday I went through more conflicting emotions than at any time since the murder of the 'Unmentionable' [Rasputin]. …
>
> [I have been] ill all to-day from overstrung nerves after the intense excitement of yesterday. People of all classes are profoundly disappointed at the tragedy of Kornilov's miscalculation. On Kornilov's approach sixty thousand workmen were armed by the Provisional Government. They keep their arms, so we are completely in their power.[17]

Stopford took to reading his tarot cards again. In a letter dated 13 September, he wrote:

> As the Kornilov attempt to bring order has failed, I will tell you what I foresee now, for the cards are shuffled again. [Kerensky] is already in the hands of the Soviet. The Soviet now have virtually all power, and the *Bolsheviki* will become more daring and try to turn out the Government; then would come anarchy, with 70,000 workmen fully armed. With the *Bolsheviki* are all the criminal classes. The failure of Kornilov has completely knocked me over, and yesterday I could not walk. I still foresee an ocean of blood before order comes.[18]

Some of the remaining grand dukes, including Dmitri's father Pavel Alexandrovich, were implicated in Kornilov's plot and quickly arrested. Stopford saw little hope that Tsarist Russia would ever be restored. He had hoped that stability might be established with the Provisional Government, but even this was not to be. On 14 September Stopford learned that the Soviet grip had grown ever tighter on the government, and Kerensky's own position was now under threat. Kornilov's failed *coup d'etat* had been the last deal of the cards and he was arrested by Kerensky.

But Stopford had also heard through General Sir Charles Barter at the Embassy that Kornilov's action against the government had not been so clear cut, and that Kerensky may have been involved in Kornilov's plot in order to establish order in the capital and suppress the anti-war propaganda being sown by the Bolsheviks.

> [Barter] had seen Kerenski during the day, if not actually to intercede for Kornilov, at least to explain the actual situation to him. There is still a mystery about the failure, but there is no doubt that Kerenski was in the *complot* with him. ... Kerenski left Kornilov in the lurch.[19]

In the wake of Kornilov's failure, the popularity of the Bolsheviks soared due to the part their supporters played in the defence of the city. The Soviet itself was now becoming infiltrated by Bolshevik members who planned to oust the existing Committee. And as the word spread of the Bolshevik gains, the soviets in the army, and in the towns and villages throughout the country, began to pass into Bolshevik hands.

Stopford feared that with the Soviet in the ascendancy, Kerensky's time was over:

> If the Soviet gets the upper hand, the Emperor may be tried, and all the Imperial family will run great risks, and peace will be made with Germany in forty-eight hours. ... No respectable person's life would be worth a couple of *sous*.[20]

* * *

Kornilov's defeat also brought Stopford face to face with his biggest challenge – getting the jewels safely out of the country. As the day of his intended return drew nearer, Yusupov was back in Petrograd on yet another mission to rescue family possessions. It is not clear whether Stopford helped him on this occasion, but it was obvious that Yusupov was taking an enormous risk by appearing so often in Petrograd at this time. Stopford was well aware of Yusupov's attraction to risk and gave him 'a good talking to',[21] advising him to leave the city as soon as possible.

With the help of his remaining servants, Felix gathered together what was left of his personal jewels and *objets d'arts* from the

Yusupov Palace, before going on to the Anichkov Palace to look for any small, valuable pieces belonging to Maria Feodorovna. Although the authorities had already located the Empress's jewels, Yusupov managed to retrieve a large portrait of her late husband, the Tsar Alexander III.

Felix then travelled to Moscow where, with his servant Gregory Boujinsky, he hid some of his diamonds in a secret recess under a staircase in his palace. Years later Yusupov discovered that both the Provisional and Bolshevik Governments had failed to locate the diamonds, and Boujinsky had never revealed their whereabouts, even under torture. Eight years later a workman discovered the jewels while repairing a step on the staircase.

From Moscow, Yusupov journeyed down to the Crimea where he broke the news to Maria Feodorovna that her jewels had been confiscated. It was of some comfort, however, that he was able to hand over the portrait of her late husband.

Stopford noted in his diary on 1 September that Maria's health had been a cause for recent concern. Although freed by Kerensky himself from the threat of night searches after an impassioned appeal from her grand-daughter Irina Yusupov, Maria was still forced to remain in the villa at Ai-Todor. She was also now aware that her son and his family were under close guard at Tobolsk.

* * *

Stopford was busy making his final plans to smuggle out the jewels he had rescued. He was familiar with the system of the British Embassy's diplomatic bags and had already couriered messages back and forth to London. But this time it was different – the contents would be unofficial. He could perhaps place the jewels in the diplomatic bag as normal and alert London to look out for them; or he could take the bag out with him in person and face the terrible risk of discovery en route. What Stopford feared most was another argument with Customs officials, and the consequent loss of the jewels, imprisonment, or even worse.

In these last few weeks another possibility had emerged. A special unit of the Royal Navy had been operating in Russia for nearly two years, and although hardly a secret operation, it was unusual. The brainchild of Commander Oliver Locker-Lampson of the Royal Navy, a colleague at the British Embassy, the British Armoured Car Division of the Royal Navy Air Service was known locally as the Russian Armoured Car Division.

Locker-Lampson's unit had a colourful past. The Navy's air arm had been active in Flanders in the early part of the war and its aircraft reconnaissance activities were supported by a unit of Lanchester armoured cars. These vehicles were fitted with a machine-gun on a small cupola on their turret roof, and had side shields for added protection. As they had more than proved their worth in action before trench warfare established itself on the Western Front, the Russian Army had ordered twenty vehicles. Locker-Lampson suggested that his squadron should not only go out with the vehicles and advise on their use, but become an integral part of the Russian Army.

Although a bold proposal, Locker-Lampson, later to become a member of parliament, lobbied his case with such conviction that the Admiralty agreed to send not just one squadron, but a full division made up of three squadrons to Russia under his command.

The division landed in the north of Russia towards the end of 1915, and until the Revolution broke out in early 1917 they were continually engaged on many fronts – especially in the Caucasus, the frontiers with Turkey and Persia, and later those of Romania and Galicia. However, the problems that had beset Russia during the late summer of 1917 had affected the work of Locker-Lampson's squadrons in the south; and as political pressure from the Bolsheviks rendered their military task more complex by the day, a decision was taken to evacuate all three squadrons.

All of this was well known to Albert Stopford through Locker-Lampson, who had been busy at the Embassy organising his division's withdrawal from Russia. It was now planned that the first men would leave from Arkhangel in the third week of August, with the remainder due to return later in groups, the last due to arrive back in Britain in February 1918.

A young man called John Stopford, who had been in Russia since the division's arrival in the country, was among the first to go. Born into an army family, his father had joined an infantry regiment in London in the early 1870s and married a London girl while on service in the West Indies. John was born in New York a few months after his father died in 1896 and was subsequently brought up in Barbados and Trinidad. After holding a job in the Royal Mail shipping group in Port of Spain, he decided at nineteen to join the forces as his father had done. After enlisting in the Royal Navy, he moved on to the newly formed Russian Armoured Car Division in November 1915.

What brought the two Stopfords together remains a mystery. Despite a common surname, their paths could not have crossed before John's arrival in Russia from the West Indies. John's children, who possess a number of Albert Stopford's belongings, have so far failed to establish a family link. Albert may have simply noticed the surname among the military papers he had access to at the Embassy, or he could have been alerted to it by one of the staff.

Before taking leave of Petrograd himself, Albert received a letter

from Maria Pavlovna in Kislovodsk, telling him that a local Committee of Workmen and Soldiers had invaded her house at 2.30 in the morning and stayed until six, 'opening, searching and turning everything topsy-turvy'.[22] She must have known that it would be of great satisfaction to Stopford, as it was to her, that he had in his possession some of the items they were searching for.

The day before his departure Stopford went out to Tsarskoe Selo to see Boris, who was very sad to see his friend leave. 'You are my last link with civilisation,'[23] Boris said as they shook hands. Stopford wished him good luck.

It now seems more than likely that Stopford's return to Britain had been arranged to coincide with John Stopford's departure. John's passport, still held by his family,[24] was issued in Petrograd on 11 September 1917 recording him as an accountant. It was stamped by the British Consulate on 25 September, granting the holder permission to travel to the United States of America. John's route was eastwards by way of Vladivostock, Yokohama, San Francisco, New York, and on to Liverpool before arriving in London. Albert Stopford left Petrograd the very next day, on 26 September, travelling in the opposite direction to London by way of Sweden.

It is now known that Albert, with the possible collusion of John, managed to bring the jewels out of Russia successfully. John's family firmly believe that their father was aware of Albert's plans.

As it turned out Stopford's journey by boat via Sweden to Aberdeen, and then by train to London, was largely uneventful, his very real fears unsubstantiated. He arrived in Aberdeen on 6 October 1917. John arrived in Liverpool on 7 January 1918.

Serge Obolensky, whose family benefited personally from Bertie's bravery, said that he had 'stuffed the jewels in a suitcase and carried them to London'.[25] Obolensky also confirmed that Stopford had been directly involved in the rescue of his own mother's jewels, as well as those of Maria Pavlovna, and he credits him with at least three additional attempts to rescue Romanov jewels and of 'doing a lot more on the side'.[26]

CHAPTER TWELVE

Trial at the Old Bailey

ALBERT Stopford left Russia on 26 September 1917 full of apprehension for the frail and fragmented Provisional Government under Alexander Kerensky. By October/November the Bolsheviks, led by Lenin, would be poised to take control, but by that time Stopford had already landed in Aberdeen, relieved and 'delighted to see policemen again'.[1] His next encounter with the police, however, was to be a rather different affair.

But for now there was real sadness to endure when Lady Gladys de Grey died on 27 October, barely weeks after his return. As the recipient of so many of his letters during his stay in Petrograd, Stopford must have been devastated that their time together was to be so brief.

Lady Gladys left her leasehold house and premises at Coombe Court to her husband for the duration of his lifetime, and thereafter to her daughter Lady Juliet Duff.[2] She also made five special bequests in memory of the success of the *Ballet Russes*. Nijinsky was given a chalk drawing of himself by the American artist John Singer Sargent, Tamara Karsavina a portrait by Glyn Philpot, and Sergei Diaghilev a fawn-coloured illustration. Close friend and neighbour Mrs Hwfa Williams was left a jade pendant on a jade chain, and her friend Bertie Stopford inherited a marble swan on a grey marble plinth and an Empire inkstand.

Stopford found a very different society in London to the one he had left behind in 1915. Having served both his Whitehall masters and Romanov friends during his years in Petrograd, he now found himself with no part to play in the new Russia as the Bolsheviks tightened their grip on the country. Equally, he had nothing much to do in London either.

Allowing himself time to recuperate from the deprivations of Petrograd, Stopford found London, despite the rationing and occasional air alert, relatively peaceful. As his health and strength gradually returned, his restless mind began to consider the possibility that his work in Russia might be resumed, although under quite different circumstances.

Having succumbed to the turmoil of the Revolution, Russia was now in the grip of a deadly civil war between the Bolshevik Red Army and a counter-revolutionary White Army that had instigated a campaign of organised resistance against the new regime. The White Army consisted mostly of liberals and ex-Tsarist officers, and other factions who considered themselves anti-Bolshevik.

Lenin's new government, re-styled the Council of the People's Commissars, was led almost exclusively through his recently established *Politbureau*, and it moved very quickly to end the war with Germany. Lenin was willing to accept almost any terms to secure peace in his attempt to consolidate the position of the Bolshevik Party (renamed the Communist Party) which was still the smallest faction in the government. The war was a distraction from Lenin's long-term plans for dictatorship, and on 3 March 1918 the Brest-Litovsk Treaty was signed in Poland between the Central Powers and the new Soviet Government. As German forces had been successful along the Eastern Front, the terms of the Treaty were inevitably harsh, and Russia lost Poland, Finland, the Baltic states, parts of Belorussia and the Caucasus, and was forced to recognise Ukraine as an independent republic.

Brest-Litovsk caused the Allied governments great concern, as Germany would now be free to pull back troops from the east to bolster the offensive along the Western Front. The Allies moved quickly to hinder Germany's withdrawal, and a strategy of intervention was organised. In 1918 France and Britain sent troops to occupy Murmansk and Arkhangel in the north of Russia. France also sent an army to the Black Sea, while Japanese soldiers moved into Vladivostock. The purpose of intervention, it was claimed, was to engage with German forces in the East, although co-operation with the White armies in these areas was an inevitable consequence.

Britain and France were also alarmed at the prospect of Germany securing commercial footholds within the vast territories forfeited by Russia over Brest-Litovsk, prompting intense discussion in Whitehall and the Quay d'Orsay. Of immediate urgency was the need for what was officially described as 'propaganda' – agents, leaflets, bribery, and so on – to offset German economic encroachment into areas of Russia such as Odessa, Kiev, and other parts of the Ukraine.[3]

Keeping up-to-date with the response of the Allies to the Treaty, Stopford realised that his dealings with Whitehall in the recent past were of less value under the Soviet regime, but his familiarity with the country might still be of use. As both the Foreign and War Offices were involved in Russia and its strategic position in terms of the outcome of the war, Stopford reacquainted himself with both departments during the spring of 1918.

The War Office was already aware of Albert Stopford, and had recently recommended him for a Meritorious Service Medal for distinguished services to the British Expeditionary Force in France during the early months of the war. He was finally deemed ineligible on 29 April 1918,[4] presumably on the legal grounds that he had not been a member of the armed forces. Although disappointed at this outcome, Stopford was still determined to approach his contacts in Whitehall to clarify whether he might still be of use to the Allies' war effort in the Russian territories.

Less than a fortnight later, on 11 May 1918, Stopford wrote from his London base at the Carlton Hotel to Lord Robert Cecil at the Foreign Office, reminding him of his previous experience in Russia:

> I am in touch with those who were in Petrograd a month ago and the point I am anxious to make is that there is still, at this present time an opportunity of starting a pro-Entente, and especially a pro-British, civilian propaganda in Russia with a fair prospect of success amongst the people and the soldiers.[5]

Lord Cecil, as Assistant Under Secretary of State and Minister of Blockade, worked closely with Colonel John Buchan who was in charge of the Department of Information and a member of MI6.

Stopford requested a brief interview, where he would be better able to explain what he had in mind. The minister was away, but as one of his colleagues knew Stopford it was agreed that a meeting would be arranged. The Foreign Office is silent on what happened next. No doubt Stopford met with Cecil, but any possibility of pursuing his proposal to get involved in pro-Entente propaganda was soon completely negated by a difficult situation of his own making.

The seeds had been sown the previous November in London in a chance encounter Stopford made in the Haymarket. Just over a month after his return from Petrograd, Stopford was staying at the Carlton Hotel, at the bottom of the Haymarket below Charles II Street. Keen to banish thoughts of the war from his mind and to explore any attractions on offer, he went out for a walk. Although the black-out was enforced, theatres and restaurants in areas such as the Haymarket and Strand still thronged with servicemen and women on leave, and the roads were busy with cars taking people out for the evening. In the middle of the crowd Stopford noticed a young Scots Guardsman salute him, and wondered if the soldier was acknowledging the King's messenger badge he was wearing.

Stopford stopped to chat. The guardsman did not appear to be with his regiment, and Stopford did not ask him about it. Instead they went for a drink, perhaps to the Waterloo Tavern on the corner of Charles II Street, or more likely to the Carlton.

Private Robert Anderson was from Aberdeen. A coal-miner by trade, he joined the army before the declaration of war in 1914. Wounded at Ypres, he had also suffered the terrible effects of a gas attack the following year.[6] Stopford found him to be good company and they chatted about many things, including the theatre, Robert Burns and sport. When Anderson expressed an interest in boxing, Stopford even arranged for lessons.

Over the next six months the two men met at the Carlton or Savoy for drinks or dinner. Anderson then took to ringing Stopford from the Bull Dog Club to arrange to meet, and over time their friendship developed. Although Stopford had enjoyed similar relationships with other soldiers in London, when Anderson announced in June that he was about to get married, Stopford was completely taken aback.

On the day of his wedding, Anderson and his bride were almost at the altar when two sergeants of the Scots Guards dramatically intervened and accused the bridegroom of already being married. This was strenuously denied by the vicar and the couple, and the wedding went ahead. But as they left the church, Anderson was seized by the sergeants, hand-cuffed and arrested on a charge of desertion.

Robert Anderson wrote frantically to his wife from his prison cell as he awaited his court martial:

> The people down here know that I knew too much, and they are hurrying things up as much as poss., so that I cannot have a dog's chance of defending myself. You know that Stopford and other people have a hold on me, and I am going to show them up, but I must have the support which is necessary at my Court Martial. I want you to go to the Editor of *John Bull* [Mr Horatio Bottomley] and let him or someone in authority read this letter and try and send someone to investigate and if possible see me. ... Stopford and others used me for their own purposes, me being under the impression that they could make things alright for me. ...[7]

Later that week Mrs Anderson arrived on the doorstep of the *John Bull* office in Longacre and handed over her husband's plea. They could not have chosen a better ally. The weekly journal was anti-establishment and at the peak of its crusade against the conduct of the war, currently berating the Prince of Wales for continuing to use his motto 'Ich Dien' on his insignia during a war against Germany, criticising the Ministry of Food for glaring inefficiency, and generally supporting the powerless classes against those in authority.

Horatio Bottomley, founder, owner and editor of *John Bull*, was an accomplished and quick-witted orator, a former member of parliament able to hold his own with the likes of Lloyd George and Winston Churchill, and capable of defending himself in open court. His exposure as a monetary fraud, liar and hypocrite was a long way into the future. But for now, as the war rumbled on, Bottomley was happy to encourage servicemen and women to vent their frustrations. And as letters from disaffected soldiers poured into his office, Bottomley did his best to follow up individual complaints vigorously, and to fill column inches on the strength of his crusades.

On the day Mrs Anderson crossed the threshold of *John Bull*, Bottomley was in the middle of his latest court action. But sensing good publicity, he turned his full attention and the journal's resources to this case of obvious injustice. From Mrs Anderson's letter, Bottomley understood that her husband had been threatened with court martial for desertion, and was claiming that two men, including a man named as Albert Stopford, had a hold over him and were the cause of his alleged desertion.

Bottomley rubbed his hands with glee – he could hardly resist such a challenge. A self-styled hero of the common man, he immediately arranged to visit Anderson. When it was established from the soldier that blackmail was involved, Bottomley agreed, on behalf of *John Bull,* to defend him at his court martial set for 1 July 1918.

Sufficient evidence for the defence was brought forward on the day of the trial to ensure that the original charge of desertion was dropped and Anderson was convicted of the lesser charges of absence without leave and losing equipment.[8] He was sentenced to six months' detention at Wandsworth Barracks, a far lighter punishment than he might otherwise have received. But this, however, was only the beginning, as Bottomley now turned his righteous indignation and column inches to the serious charges brought against Albert Stopford and another man similarly accused, named as Cecil Arthur Samter and described as an officer in the Royal Air Force.

The first shot in Bottomley's locker was fired on 20 July 1918, under the lurid headline 'Vice and the Victim; The Scots Guard and the Blackguards':

> ... Men of position, one a King's Messenger, got hold of this young fellow for their own evil purposes, and by throwing the cloak of their influence over him made it possible for him to absent himself from his regiment for months. It was not until they realised that he was done with their decadent and degrading ways – that lavish presents; that visits to one man's rooms at the Carlton Hotel and to another at the Premier Hotel in Russell Square; that dinners here and luncheons there could not be set against his affection for an honest woman, that they turned upon him. They knew him to be a deserter ... and yet from November 1917 to June 1918 they were parties to his offence against discipline. But his reformation meant

their anger. How came it that after seven months' immunity in London this young private was arrested at his wedding. ... Yes, there is a greater fury than the fury of a woman scorned![9]

John Bull also revealed statements given in evidence at the court martial. Anderson, it seemed, had been walking around London in uniform for seven months unchallenged, and had even on occasion returned to his barracks at Wellington Square. He had lunched with various well-positioned gentlemen at fashionable restaurants and been known to have access to the War Office late at night to areas referred to as the inner sanctuary. As a private soldier absent without leave, Robert Anderson was surely taking some very great risks.

The article also said that *John Bull* had letters in its possession concerning the true nature of the relationship between Anderson, Stopford and Cecil Samter, which they had offered to the police. It would be up to the authorities, the article inferred, to establish the identity of those who had provided the information which led to the arrest, imprisonment and detention of the Scots Guardsman – the implication being that it was Stopford, Samter, or both.

The following week *John Bull* provided details of what Private Anderson had said under oath, and in answer to pertinent questions from counsel about Cecil Arthur Samter's conduct:

Counsel: Did [Cecil Samter] tell you that if you did that and went away out of his company, he would inform anybody, or anything of that sort?
Anderson: Yes he threatened me from time to time.
Counsel: Threatened you with what?
Anderson: Threatened me that if I could not let him have my company he would give me away to the military authorities.[10]

It was also revealed by *John Bull* that Samter, although mostly found in mufti or civilian clothes, wore an officer's badge and possessed a pass which entitled him to call on the military or civil police for protection, implying, rightly or wrongly, that he was a member of the secret service.

John Bull also added that Stopford and Samter were not the only known associates of Private Anderson. The article went on to list a 'Lieutenant-Surgeon on one of His Majesty's ships', an 'Army Captain' who was an Inspector of Canteens, a 'Major in the Coldstream Guards', a 'Captain in the Wiltshire regiment', and a 'Lieutenant in the Air Force', among those responsible for the 'undoing of this private soldier'.[11]

John Bull was morally outraged about Anderson being taken advantage of, and called for punitive action. 'If our facts are facts,'

104

the article thundered, 'then it is the duty of the authorities to act without further hesitation.'[12]

Albert Stopford did not escape *John Bull's* invective:

> It is true that certain inquiries have been made of us, but where the character and honour of a King's Messenger are concerned there is no room for red-tape. Either this man Stopford is reputable or he is not. We declare him not to be, by his vile practices and evil reputation – he is notorious in certain coteries of the West End of London – unfitted for the confidential and often dangerous office of a King's Messenger. Surely this man, who is employed by the Foreign Office, should be at once suspended from his duties pending further inquiries.[13]

Stopford's notoriety in the West End at that time has more recently been alluded to in *The Duff Cooper Diaries* (2006), in which Alfred Duff Cooper wrote about being driven home by Stopford after a dinner party in Upper Berkeley Street, towards the end of 1917. 'He is a notorious bugger,' Cooper said, 'and was very attentive to me.'[14]

Official government reaction to *John Bull's* revelations was swift. The Foreign Office indicated that Albert Stopford was not a member of their staff. And a communication to *John Bull* from Windsor Castle made it clear that the same Albert Stopford was not an official King's messenger. The War Office began its own investigation into the matter, but issued no denials – a significant omission given the circumstances. In the end, the matter was taken up by the Criminal Investigation Department of Scotland Yard.

What Stopford was feeling is probably not difficult to imagine – shock, fear, utter dismay. Making the decision to meet his enemy face to face, he called round to the *John Bull* office. But unable to see Bottomley in person, he resorted to writing a letter from the Carlton:

> I haven't the pleasure of knowing you. I have been this afternoon to see you about an article which appeared in last week's number of *John Bull*. I hoped to be able to give you my version, which differs from what was published, but as I could not see you I would like to say that your interest in the Scots Guardsman is identical with mine, and I think I should have been able to help you.
>
> Yours faithfully,
> *A. Stopford*
>
> PS. If you would like to see me, you have only to telephone to me, Carlton Hotel, and I will come.[15]

When Stopford finally met Bottomley he adopted a conciliatory tone, agreeing with the journal's concern for the man's welfare. When questioned about taking a private soldier to top restaurants and entertaining him at the Carlton, Stopford tried to elicit understanding. 'Ah, I thought you would say that, but a man who went through the revolution in Petrograd loses all sense of social distinction'.[16] He was, he insisted, only taking an interest in the welfare of wounded soldiers, and he had no idea that Anderson was a deserter, since he always saw him at night when he would be out on leave anyway. When questioned about the letter Anderson had sent to his wife, Stopford claimed that the soldier had not written the letter, and even suggested that his own name had been added by someone else.

Stopford and Bottomley found little common ground on the matter and Stopford had to accept that he was not making his case any easier. Indeed it was to get much worse. With such serious accusations hanging over him he could not go abroad, presumably back to Russia, on the propaganda mission he had proposed to the Foreign Office only months earlier. *John Bull*, meanwhile, lost no time in launching another attack on Stopford and Samter the following week, in even stronger terms:

> Albert Stopford. This man, who resides at the Carlton Hotel, London, and is an official Courier, I charge with being a person of depraved and debased sexual proclivities, and a defiler of young men in the King's Army, whom he has aided and abetted to become deserters for the gratification of his own foul lust. I say that he should be dismissed from the public service and put on trial.

Bottomley ended by stating that he was using his position as Editor 'with the deliberate object of hounding such creatures as Stopford and Samter out of social life'.[17]

Neither Stopford nor Samter felt able to respond to such a deliberate challenge by initiating libel actions against *John Bull*. They may well have been advised not to do so. Instead they faced charges when the police passed evidence against them to the Public Prosecutor. Albert Henry Stopford and Cecil Arthur Samter were summoned to appear at Bow Street Magistrates Court,[18] and subsequently to attend separate trials at the Old Bailey.

Stopford's Bow Street appearance came up at the beginning of September 1918. He was accused of 'serious offences with a Scots Guardsman', and described as being 'of independent means'[19] and living in Paris. Cecil Samter, who was from Manchester, was similarly accused and both cases were passed to the Old Bailey. The trials took place a few weeks apart in November.

It seems strange that the authorities chose not to use the evidence gathered by *John Bull* during their defence of Anderson at his court martial. Perhaps there was a reluctance to pry closely into the inner workings of the armed services during a time of war. Or perhaps, as in the opinion of Travers Humphrey, Treasury Counsel at the Central

Criminal Court, Bottomley's evidence would have been difficult to prove conclusively in court.

Cecil Samter was the first to be tried. He was found guilty of committing acts of gross indecency, not guilty of other offences, and sentenced to nine months' hard labour at Wormwood Scrubs.

Albert Stopford appeared a few weeks later before Mr Justice Lawrence, accused of 'improper behaviour towards Robert Anderson and gross indecency with a male person'.[20]

Stopford pleaded not guilty, insisting rather implausibly, as he had done during his first conversation with Bottomley, that his only interest had been in the welfare of men in the services. He had thought that Robert Anderson would be discharged because he had been gassed, and never suspected that the soldier was absent without leave. Stopford touched on his own background as evidence of his good character, mentioning his friendship with the Secretary of State for War, Lord Milner (whom he had met in Petrograd), his grandfather's rank as Colonel of the Scots Guards, and his many officer friends in the Guards. He even hinted that he was prevented from going abroad on an important mission for the Foreign Office until this case had been dealt with.

Ironically, this time all his extolling of friends and acquaintances in high places was to no avail. Albert Henry Stopford was found guilty of 'committing acts of gross indecency with a male person' and sentenced to twelve months' hard labour in Wormwood Scrubs.[21] The police further revealed in court that a warrant had been issued previously for Stopford's arrest on a similar charge in connection with a Scots Guardsman in Windsor in 1894, although the said warrant had been withdrawn in 1897. Stopford's past had finally caught up with him.

From the luxury of the Carlton, and the association of powerful politicians and society friends, Stopford now found himself reduced to the dreary, energy-sapping life of hard labour in prison. Smart suits were swapped for penitential grey, and his freedom to walk limited to a single-file circle within the prison grounds for one hour in the day. There would be few visits, no books, and endless solitary confinement.

Stopford's characteristic resilience was now tested to its limit. But what really hit him with a body blow was the criticism and lack of sympathy from the majority of his erstwhile friends who deserted him at the first sign of public disgrace. On his release from prison the following year, he finally began to understand who his real friends were.

**QUEEN ALEXANDRA AND EMPRESS MARIA
FEODOROVNA, MAY 1919**

Queen Alexandra (1844-1925) (left), widow of King
Edward VII, with her sister (middle), the Dowager
Empress Maria Feodorovna of Russia (1847-1928),
photographed at the Chelsea Flower Show in 1919,
soon after Maria had left Russia as a refugee.

(© Hulton Archive/Topical Press Agency/
Getty Images)

CHAPTER THIRTEEN

The Last
Romanov Émigré

O N the day Albert Stopford left Wormwood Scrubs in 1919, he was greeted by Serge Obolensky and Juliet Duff who were among the few who had kept in touch when others had drifted away. They took Stopford back to an apartment he sometimes used in St James's Square, a *pied-a-terre* owned by a senior member of the Foreign Office, and gave him time to get used to his freedom. It was clear that recent events had taken their toll and Bertie looked far from well. Prison life had been very hard for him, more so perhaps than his time in Petrograd, or his public humiliation in the press. Mentally and physically he had deteriorated.

Many years later Serge Obolensky, looking back on the effect of that decade on so many of his friends, had this to say about Stopford:

> I often thought of Bertie Stopford who had taken greater risks for a longer period of time than almost everyone else I knew, a cheerful, hearty, healthy individual who really enjoyed facing incalculable dangers from the Bolsheviks. Somehow he had miraculously escaped, but then, safe in London, with everything in the world to live for, an almost Proustian climax ended his career – or anticlimax, for there seemed nothing for him to do. He was bored and restless and the world of peace had become a prolonged waste of time whose dullness caused him infinite trouble as he struggled against it.[1]

Their meeting on the day he left prison was a profoundly painful occasion. 'Bertie,' Obolensky said, 'had braved the gunmen of the *Cheka* without a moment's hesitation, but the censure of his supposed friends was too much. He told us so. It was tragic and we knew then he had to go away.'[2]

Before going to prison, Stopford had been working on a book based on the diary he kept in Petrograd and the letters sent to individuals such as Lady Gladys de Grey and Lady Sarah Wilson. It was Countess Betsy Schuvalov (formerly Princess Baritinsky, a friend of Maria Pavlovna) who persuaded him to publish his writings, and he approached the company William Heinemann to test their interest. Heinemann agreed to publish and the book came out anonymously four months after Stopford entered Wormwood Scrubs. The negative publicity generated by *John Bull,* and the subsequent jail sentence, probably accounted for the absence of his name. Another interesting consequence of the trial was the changing of the original title from *Diary of an Official Diplomatiste* to *The Russian Diary of an Englishman.*

Stopford was acutely aware that the British authorities had distanced themselves from his work in Russia by denying that he had held any official post. With his future now looking so uncertain, Stopford chose to take a lump sum in lieu of any royalties from his publisher. He also left no forwarding address.[3]

But it was the lingering disapproval of some of his closest friends in London that continued to affect Stopford profoundly. 'Soon after [our meeting],' Obolensky wrote, 'he left for the Continent. He never returned.'[4] Stopford had spent twenty years of his life in Paris, and was in the capital when war broke out. It was time to move on, and to pick up his past career in the world of antiques and *objets d'art,* away from London and his recent troubles.

During Stopford's brief excursions to Paris from Petrograd, he had often stayed at the Hôtel Lotti in the rue Castiglione, but following his final departure from London he took up residence in the apartment at 31 rue de Valois in the Palais Royal which he had used since 1911. The Palais Royal was originally approved by Louis XVI, and the apartments situated on the upper floors overlook the magnificent gardens below. Stopford's living area, with its entrance into rue de Valois, was on the side opposite the Bank of France.

Back in Paris, Stopford took stock of his situation and resolved to meet up with a few of Maria Pavlovna's friends and to renew his correspondence with her in the Caucasus. Having been out of circulation for an entire year at Wormwood Scrubs, so much had changed and he was already aware of the terrible hardships that had befallen so many of his Russian friends.

When Tsar Nicholas II abdicated in March 1917 there were fifty-three members of the Romanov family resident in Russia. One died of natural causes in Tashkent in 1918, but of the fifty-two who remained seventeen were murdered at the hands of militant soviets or on government orders. In April and May 1918 the Imperial family and their servants, under pressure from the soviet at Ekaterinburg, had been moved in two separate groups from Tobolsk to Ekaterinburg where a local house had been requisitioned for them. A special detachment of soldiers, under Commissar Y. Y. Yakovlev, was then sent to look after them. The house, known as the Ipatiev house after its owner, had been codenamed the 'House of Special Purpose'. It was fenced off from view and heavily guarded.

By May of 1918 the Treaty of Brest-Litovsk had caused Czech

soldiers to withdraw from Russia through Vladivostock, ready to relocate to the Western Front to fight for Czechoslovakian independence. But when the soldiers became embroiled in an incident with the Red Army south of Ekaterinburg, they were ordered to disarm or be shot. Refusing to do so, the Czechs moved instead against Ekaterinburg, threatening the area where the Imperial family was detained. Leon Trotsky, Minister of War under Lenin, and in charge of the Red Army, was aware that if the White Army gained access to the family through the Czechs, Nicholas could be used as a figurehead to rally support. The Red Army was not yet ready to withstand such a force.

The story of how Nicholas, Alexandra, their children and servants were killed in the Ipatiev House on 16/17 July 1918, on the authority of the Bolsheviks, has been told many times. The most authentic account, however, was written by Edvard Radzinsky, the Russian playwright, who based his version of events on the original report of the Commandant of the Ipatiev House, Y. M. Yurovsky, who described what happened in the cellar of the 'House of Special Purpose':

> [Yurovsky] ... instantly pulled a revolver out of his pocket and shot the tsar. The [tsarina] and her daughter Olga tried to make the sign of the cross, but did not have enough time.
>
> Nich[olas] was killed by the commandant, point blank. Then A[lexandra] F[eodorovna] died immediately.
>
> [Alexei], three of his sisters, the lady in waiting [Dermitov] and [Dr] Botkin were still alive. They had to be finished off.[5]

In addition to the Tsar's immediate family, his brother Mikhail Alexandrovich was shot in June 1918 at Perm. Elizaveta Feodorovna, the sister of Alexandra, Sergei Mikhailovich, a cousin of Nicholas II, Princes of the Imperial Blood Ioann and Kostantin Konstantinovich, and Prince Vladimir Pavlovich Paley, the young son of Pavel Alexandrovich, were among those clubbed in the head and thrown down a well-shaft at Alapaevsk in the Urals in July of the same year. In January 1919, on the orders of the All-Russian Extraordinary Commission, Nicholai Mikhailovich, Georgy Mikhailovich and Dmitri Konstantinovich were executed in the Peter and Paul Fortress in Petrograd. Dmitri Pavlovich's father, Pavel Alexandrovich, was also shot on that day.

*   *   *

Other Romanovs were more fortunate and managed to escape before the bloodshed began. The first of the extended family to leave Russia was Maria Pavlovna's son Kyril Vladimirovich. Considered loyal to the Provisional Government, Kyril, his wife Victoria Melita, and two daughters, arrived in Finland in June 1917. As Victoria was pregnant, they left Russia by train complete with two English nurses and a large amount of luggage, including some of their own jewels.

Thereafter the various Romanovs who had taken refuge in the Crimea were, as Stopford discovered, under intermittent house arrest or at the mercy of local factions. But with the rise of the Red Army in a country so vast and divided, the violence was unpredictable, and the exiled families soon found themselves caught between competing soviets in Yalta and Sebastopol, intent on either murdering or defending their former rulers. Later the Romanovs would be saved by the encroachment of German troops in the wake of Brest-Litovsk, but even this phase did not last. Following the Allied defeat of Germany in November 1918 that signalled the end of the war, the Red Army emerged once again to threaten the area.

With the war now over, Britain's Queen Alexandra intervened swiftly to help her sister Maria Feodorovna. King George had despatched an immediate message of sympathy after the abdication, although it did not get to Nicholas, and later made an offer to grant the family asylum in Britain for the duration of the war. This offer was withdrawn in April 1917, however, as George became concerned about the affect on his own position and the vulnerability of his coalition government if the Imperial family was to be brought to Britain. With anti-German feeling running so high in Britain, and the rumblings of socialism on the increase, the Tsar and his family would have proved a serious political and security risk. But by the end of 1918, painfully aware of what had happened to the Romanovs, and aware too of the escalation of Red Army skirmishes in the Crimea and surrounding area, George moved quickly to ensure that his mother's sister did not suffer the same fate.

The Admiralty, with the approval of the British Government, sent a secret signal to the Commander-in-Chief, Mediterranean, to get ready to send a ship to the Crimea to bring Maria Feodorovna and her family out of Russia. On 21 November 1918 a British naval officer arrived just north of Ai-Todor to assess the Empress's current situation and found Maria reluctant to leave, clinging on to the belief that her son and his family were still alive. In an Admiralty message despatched to King George, the Royal Navy reported the following:

> Audience with Empress Maria. Offered to take her to Constantinople. She is in good health. No anxiety (not shared by her entourage). From enquiries she had caused to be made, she is of the opinion that the Emperor may be still alive and on that account wishes to remain in Russia.[6]

It took further persuasion from her sister in London, and more evidence of the Red Army's increasing dominance in the area, to convince Maria that it was dangerous to remain. Even so, it was April 1919 before she agreed to leave – and only if permitted to bring others out with her.

The refugees finally left Russia on 11 April 1919 in two British naval vessels, HMS *Marlborough* and HMS *Nelson*. Maria Feodorovna was accompanied by her daughter Xenia and her husband Alexander Mikhailovich. Nicholas Nicholaevich, the former Commander-in-Chief, and his brother Peter were also among their number, as well as Felix and Irina Yusupov, with members of the Yusupov family. After a brief stay in Malta, Maria travelled on to London to be with her sister, while the Yusupovs made their way through Genoa to Paris.

* * *

The Grand Duchess Maria Pavlovna, still detained in Kislovodsk, was the last Romanov to leave Russia after the Revolution. Although the civil war between the Red and White armies continued around the major cities, Kislovodsk had remained relatively undisturbed until January 1918 when the first Red Army troops appeared. They immediately closed the banks, post office and telephone exchange, and arrested local officers:

> Kislovodsk was not taken over all at once by the Bolsheviks, but gradually. An armoured train would suddenly arrive with its band of Red Guards and commissars and then depart again, and a period of relative calm would follow this upheaval.[7]

The comfort of close friends, combined with the temporary successes of the White Army and rumours of a counter-revolution, had encouraged Maria to remain in the Caucasus. But towards the end of 1918 the disturbing incursions of Red Army soldiers onto her estate began to escalate. A mission from the Bolsheviks arrived one day unannounced with the sole intention of raising thousands of roubles from its inhabitants, although there was clearly little money to be had. And on another occasion Red Army soldiers entered the villa intent on finding jewels. Maria was with her attendant Princess Turia Galitzine and caught sight of the soldiers as they approached. She whispered to Turia to continue with her sewing and to say and do nothing: 'We must be resolute and not look up.' The men walked around the room as the two ladies kept their heads down and continued with their work, ignoring the questions and instructions fired at them. Two of the soldiers began to argue with each other: 'You said *you* would shoot them' – 'No, *you* should do it.'[8] The soldiers left as suddenly as they had appeared.

The most aggressive incursion ended in the arrest of Maria's sons Andrei and Boris. Although released quickly on the intervention of a friendly commissar, they now understood the seriousness of their predicament and went into hiding in the area for a couple of months.

Such sporadic Red Army disturbances were soon followed by the occasional successes of the White Army, as the tide of war swayed backwards and forwards around the refugees from Petrograd. By October 1918, however, the Red Army was in the ascendancy and Maria, her sons and countless other refugees began a long exodus from Kislovodsk – in cars, on horseback, in wagons and on foot. Maria was advised to divert to the Black Sea coast at Anapa until the situation settled down in the Caucasus, and this would become their home for the next six months.

Anapa, though a temporary haven, came as a shock to the Grand Duchess. Although food was plentiful, she had few clothes and little money to live on. Writing a letter to a friend in Paris, she complained that basic comforts were 'unknown, such as W.C.s and baths'. She later looked back on it as 'that awful hole'.[9] Increasingly apprehensive – and aware that Maria Feodorovna and her relatives were being similarly treated in the Crimea – Maria, Andrei, Boris and her sons' partners began to look for possible avenues of escape.

Maria sought the advice of General Frederick Poole, the former British military representative in Petrograd, who was now in Constantinople. Poole made a difficult six-hour journey in what he later described as a 'most terrible boat'[10] to meet in secret with Maria and her sons at Anapa. On arrival, much to his horror, he was greeted by an excited, cheering crowd who saw his visit as a preliminary to an Allied military expedition to protect them from the Bolsheviks. To avoid suspicion, Poole claimed to be in the area to consider locations for a military hospital.

General Poole met with Maria Pavlovna over lunch and they discussed her chances of escape. He found her brave and charming, although obviously shaken by her experiences. Poole's advice was to get out of Russia immediately, and he promised to contact London about getting visas for Britain. Similar applications from Romanovs in the Crimea were already under consideration, although London had not granted entry to all of them. Poole also indicated that he would wire for a ship to come for them as soon as it was required.[11]

If Maria impressed the General, Boris Vladimirovich did not. Poole found him 'cold-footed and a thoroughly useless fellow'.[12] This judgment was more than shared by the Foreign Office, where two senior officials minuted Boris's application thus:

'Ought not Lord Stamfordham [the King's private secretary] to be consulted before we reply?'

'We know H.M.'s [His Majesty's] wishes on the subject. Reply that it is regretted that permission cannot be granted at the present moment'.

'I agree. He is no good.'[13]

Often outspoken in his criticism of the British Army, and usually in the presence of British military officers, Boris's comments had not gone unnoticed in London. Spurned by Whitehall, Boris took a boat to France with his mistress Zinaida Rashevskaya within a matter of weeks of being refused entry. The couple eventually relocated to Nice.

Maria, Andrei and his mistress Mathilde Kschessinska, a former prima ballerina of the Imperial Ballet, made a decision not to depart at this time. Nonetheless, a British cruiser appeared off the coast of Anapa, sent by Admiral Seymour of the British Black Sea Squadron to escort the family to Constantinople in the event of danger. Commander Goldschmidt, in charge of the cruiser, was informed by Maria that she considered it her duty to remain in Russia and only to leave in the case of absolute necessity. Goldschmidt could only admire her resolve.

One reason behind Maria's reluctance to leave was the apparent success of the White Army. There were rumours in the town of the possible fall of Moscow to the Whites, and such optimism, although unfounded, encouraged the remaining refugees in Anapa to return to Kislovodsk. By the end of May 1919 Maria Pavlovna was back where she started, using her characteristic ingenuity to establish every means of communication possible. With American, Swedish and French contacts acting as go-betweens, she began writing endless letters to friends and family in Petrograd and Paris.

One recipient of her letters to the French capital was Alexander Ouchakoff, the son of General Paul Ouchakoff, who was inundated with a stream of Maria's complaints, requests and family gossip. Ouchakoff, who had settled in Paris back in 1910, was in touch with Maria's friends in the city, including her favourite French jeweller Cartier. In one of the letters Maria described her life in Kislovodsk, bemoaning her declined circumstances:

> I am resigned to hardship. ... At my age it's hard to sleep in a bad bed, not to have enough linen, clothes, no baths, no dresses or furs for the winter and to eat badly.[14]

Ouchakoff was also on the receiving end of her strident outpourings concerning Boris and his, to her mind, unsuitable choice of partner. Boris, having left Russia, had not been allowed to enter

France at that time and was with Zenaida in Rapallo, northern Italy. Maria was merciless in her condemnation of his mistress. In July 1919 she complained, 'she's noisy, common, ugly, stupid, bad, undesirable and unshowable in decent society. … If he is still in the clutches of that monster of a woman, anything could happen'.[15] The couple had already married in Genoa four days earlier.

When Maria asked Ouchakoff to sell a car she had bought in Paris in 1913, he managed to get nine thousand francs for it from Felix Yusupov. Although this helped to pay for a few necessities, it would hardly have pleased Maria to imagine 'Felix, the assassin'[16] driving around the French capital in her motor-car.

Ouchakoff was also urged to send various purchases to Maria – including books, magazines, clothing, a Swan pen, and even a Petit Larousse dictionary. A number of Parisian shops, it seemed, were still willing to provide the Grand Duchess with credit.

It was Ouchakoff who helped Maria to re-establish contact with Albert Stopford. Thereafter references to Stopford appeared occasionally in Maria's correspondence until in mid-November, quite surprisingly, she mentioned that Stopford was actually with her in person in Kislovodsk. Dated '17/30 November, 1919' [O.S./N.S.], she wrote to Ouchakoff, 'I'm sending you this letter through our friend Stopford who has just spent a week with me and can give you all the latest news about me and the Caucasus'.[17]

How Albert Stopford, *persona non grata* with Whitehall, had managed to sneak back into Russia, especially to Kislovodsk, remains something of mystery. But however he had managed to get into the country, it gave him the opportunity to reassure Maria that her jewels were safely locked up in a bank vault in London. And with the jewels acting as collateral for loans, she now had adequate funds should she decide to leave Russia.

In the letter to Ouchakoff couriered to Paris by Stopford, Maria betrayed her anxiety about additional money she had tried to send from London to Stockholm that autumn.[18] Countess Benckendorff, widow of the former Russian Ambassador to London, had transferred the equivalent of 100,000 kroner from the Grand Duchess's new account in London to a bank in Stockholm in the name of 'Maria Pavlovna' (Maria had given the Russian Ambassador in Stockholm power of attorney over her deposit). The intention was to have the money transferred to Ouchakoff in Paris, who would then pass the money on to Boris Vladimirovich in Rapallo. With Stopford acting as a go-between, she was able to fulfil this complex financial transaction long before her departure from Russia.

As the respite from Red Army attacks in Kislovodsk was to last little more than six months, Maria's small party was forced to move once again. This time they were to leave Russia for ever. It may have

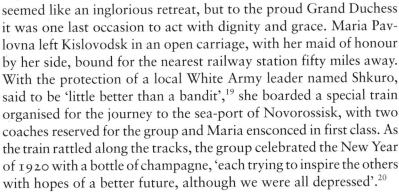

seemed like an inglorious retreat, but to the proud Grand Duchess it was one last occasion to act with dignity and grace. Maria Pavlovna left Kislovodsk in an open carriage, with her maid of honour by her side, bound for the nearest railway station fifty miles away. With the protection of a local White Army leader named Shkuro, said to be 'little better than a bandit',[19] she boarded a special train organised for the journey to the sea-port of Novorossisk, with two coaches reserved for the group and Maria ensconced in first class. As the train rattled along the tracks, the group celebrated the New Year of 1920 with a bottle of champagne, 'each trying to inspire the others with hopes of a better future, although we were all depressed'.[20]

Maria Pavlovna's arrival in Novorossisk was witnessed by her niece, Olga Alexandrovna:

> For all the dangers and privations, she still appeared every inch a Grand Duchess. There had never been much love lost between Aunt Miechen and my own family, but I felt proud of her. Disregarding peril and hardship she stubbornly kept to all the trimmings of bygone splendour and glory. And somehow she carried it off. When generals found themselves lucky to find a horse and cart to bring them to safety, Aunt Miechen made a long journey in her own train.[21]

But the ordeal was far from over, and while waiting for a ship to take her to Europe Maria was forced to spend her last six weeks in Russia in the confines of her railway compartment.

When the *Semiranisa*, a ship bound for Venice, docked in the port, Maria managed to secure a special cabin on board, and she and the others sailed for Italy on 13 February 1920. But the real plight of their situation soon became apparent, for there was little ready money between them to pay for the passage. Maria offered to use one of the remaining brooches in her possession to set against their fares, but most of her fellow travellers would never be in a position to pay her back.[22]

A month later, after a brief stopover in Constantinople, the ship docked at Piraeus, the main port of Athens. Maria took the opportunity to visit Helen's deserted house and picked three bunches of violets from the garden to take to her daughter in Switzerland. Helen had been forced into exile when her husband's brother Constantine abdicated in 1917 under the combined threat of his Prime Minister Eftherias Venizelos and his own son Alexander of Greece. Helen and Nicholas and their family had found their way to Switzerland and remained there until 1920 when Constantine was briefly reinstated as king.

Maria's long journey was now approaching its end as the *Semiranisa* sailed through the Corinth Canal and on to Venice where it cast anchor directly opposite the Doges Palace. As Maria disembarked,

Albert Stopford was waiting for her on the quayside. 'The good Stopford received us in Venice with money to pay for our ship's passage,'[23] she wrote in a letter to Ouchakoff, and it can only be imagined how emotional their meeting must have been.

Andrei Vladimirovich and Mathilde Kschessinska went out to dine in Venice on their first evening of freedom, while Stopford and Maria chose to talk in peace and quiet. There was a lot to say about the recent past, but perhaps more to consider about the future, especially in relation to the jewels rescued from the Vladimir Palace.

Maria, Andrei and Mathilde eventually travelled from Venice to the South of France on a train arranged by the Italian Government. From there they went their separate ways, with Maria taking up residence in the Grand Hôtel in Cannes.

Andrei and Mathilde went to the family villa in Cap d'Ail. Andrei had fortunately left some luggage and clothes in the villa when he last visited and had a reasonable wardrobe to start his new life. Mathilde, on the other hand, arrived with only two sets of clothes to her name. Since their retained servants and gardener would need to be paid, Andrei was forced to mortgage the villa to raise funds.[24]

At last Maria was able to spend precious time with Helen and her grand-daughters in Montreux, and the children remembered with affection their grandmother's determination to plan their future 'coming-out balls' in the Winter Palace, regardless of the ongoing turmoil in Russia. Writing about her last meeting with her grandmother, Princess Olga noticed how thin Maria had become. It was no good wondering what might have been any more – it was best to 'let dreams lie …'.[25]

In Montreux, Maria's thoughts turned to the future and to the question of inheritance. She was relieved to know that her jewels were safe and would soon be made available to her. Maria and Stopford had already discussed how and when to have them valued professionally, and whether to do so in London or Paris. Stopford had set in motion tentative arrangements for London, and Maria was inclined to agree, since any attempt to get them valued in Paris would inevitably generate publicity or gossip about her intention to sell them.

In the end the scales were tipped in favour of Cartier in Paris – a pragmatic decision, as Maria had purchased the majority of her most valuable jewels from the French jeweller. More pertinent to her current situation, however, Cartier offered to provide an estimate without charge.

Maria indicated to Stopford in a particularly heart-felt letter in mid-June 1920 that Cartier's offer was 'very tempting'. The letter began with 'My Dear Stoppy' and ended with a genuine thank you for 'all the care and trouble you take to please me'.[26] It was kind

recognition of his loyalty over the years, and it may well have been the last letter he received from 'his Grand Duchess'. It ended with promises to meet up in Paris to confirm their final decision.

In July, Andrei received a worrying telegram summoning him to his mother's bedside. Suffering terrible kidney pains, Maria had gone for respite to Contrexeville, a French spa town and one of her favourite places for rest and recuperation. The town had always held a special place in her heart and she had personally supported the building of a Russian Orthodox chapel there in 1910. With many friends still in the area, she received a warm welcome when she established herself in her favourite apartments in the Hôtel de la Souveraine.[27]

But the pains in her back grew worse, and by the time Boris, Andrei and Helen joined her in Contrexeville it was clear that an operation would be necessary to remove an abscess on her kidney. After the procedure was performed, Andrei stayed with his mother for a month while she convalesced, before he returned to Cap d'Ail.

A second telegram summoned the family once again, with Kyril this time. Maria was getting weaker by the day and was in acute pain. She died in the Hôtel de la Souveraine at dawn on 6 September 1920.[28]

The Grand Duchess Maria Pavlovna was buried in the Orthodox chapel at Contrexeville. A plaque commemorating her visits was placed above the door of her hotel suite, although it was later removed when the Germans occupied the area during the Second World War.

With the passing of Maria, the jewels that Albert Stopford had so gallantly saved became the main subject of her last will and testament.

CHAPTER FOURTEEN

The Jewels

THE Grand Duchess's original jewels were a gift from her late husband Grand Duke Vladimir and were first valued at the time of their marriage in 1874. They consisted of 244 separate pieces and included one tiara with stars and diamonds, a five-row pearl necklace with 311 pearls, another three-row necklace with 166 pearls, as well as 12 rings, 38 bracelets, 44 brooches and 52 medallions. This was only the beginning of her collection, however, and she acquired more pieces in St Petersburg, London and Paris over the years. At the turn of the twentieth century Vladimir also bought his wife four separate sets of jewellery to be bequeathed to their children – Kyril, Boris, Andrei and Helen – on her death. Each set was created from different sets of stones consisting of rubies, sapphires, emeralds and pearls.

On Vladimir's death in 1909 Maria inherited a widow's income, the equivalent of Vladimir's allocation as a grand duke, amounting to 280,000 roubles (*c.*£28,000 in pre-First World War pounds and *c.*£1,598,000 today). To this was added the Grand Duke's entire allowance as a former Commander-in-Chief of the Russian Army. It was little wonder then that trips to Fabergé and Cartier were a regular occurrence for Maria on her European travels.

Maria Pavlovna's collection had not gone unnoticed over the years. It was customary for a Russian hostess to show off her jewellery to honoured female guests, a habit that a few western Europeans, and Americans, found somewhat lacking in taste. Although Maria had been brought up in Germany, she readily adopted this particular Russian tradition, and in doing so ensured that a number of descriptions of her jewels were noted down by guests over the years.

The American heiress Consuela Vanderbilt, later the Duchess of Marlborough, was clearly taken by Maria Pavlovna, as well as her jewels, on a visit to St Petersburg:

> She had a majestic personality, but could be both gracious and charming. After dinner she showed me her jewels set out in glass cases in her dressing room. There were endless parures of diamonds, emeralds,

rubies and pearls to say nothing of semi-precious stones such as turquoises, tourmalines, cat's eyes and aquamarines.[1]

The glass cases were set into the four corners of her dressing-room, with red stones (rubies), blue (sapphires), green (emeralds) and white (pearls) in each corner, giving the room an almost octagonal appearance. Her grandchildren – Princesses Olga, Marina and Elizabeth – remembered their visits as small girls to the Vladimir Palace, and especially the inner sanctum of their grandmother's dressing-room. To amuse the girls Maria would often invite them to choose what jewels she should wear for her next formal occasion. Red, perhaps? Or blue, green or white? Olga, the eldest, usually made the final choice.[2]

Sometimes the girls would play in a specially-built house in the garden, where they were often cajoled by the adults to prepare tea for the company. Their grandmother would ring a bell inside the palace to announce that she and her guests were ready for refreshment. The bell was jewel-encrusted and made by Fabergé.

Princess Marina, later to become the Duchess of Kent, had particular reason to remember her last visit to her grandmother in St Petersburg. It was in the summer of 1914 when she was just seven years old. A vivid memory remained of her grandmother dressed magnificently in her court costume with a long train, wearing a traditional Russian head-dress or *kokoschnik*. Marina clapped her hands in delight and asked if she could try it on. Maria laughed, took the *kokoschnik* off, and bent down to place it gently on the little girl's head. Glancing round to look at herself in a mirror, Marina wanted one just like it. Her grandmother promised that she would, but not until she was older.[3]

Princess Marina did not receive the *kokoschnik*, but she and the Kent family, and her sisters, would eventually inherit some of their grandmother's exquisite jewels.

*　*　*

On Maria Pavlovna's death the family was faced with a number of immediate problems. Their mother's debts at her London bank still had to be settled and inheritance taxes paid. Each member of the family, however, was experiencing their own monetary difficulties. The jewels created additional problems as the value of the stones (rubies, sapphires, emeralds and pearls) had not kept pace with each other, and the sets of stones allocated to each of her children were worth vastly different amounts. The emeralds were at the time of valuation worth at least ten times more than the sapphires since Grand Duke Vladimir purchased them. Pearls in particular had decreased in value, in response to recent growth in supplies from Japan. Such discrepancies had to be taken into account.

On the matter of inheritance tax, as such duties were lower in Switzerland than London, lawyers advised the family to transfer the jewels that were to be sold off to Geneva. And in the late autumn of 1920, the jewels were placed in the hands of Cartier for valuation as planned, where they were individually assessed and photographed. (Albums containing the records are still kept in the Cartier archives.)[4]

In raising the monetary value from the sale of certain items of Maria's jewellery, there was a natural reluctance to involve a public auction. Through Cartier's contacts and the family's own wide inter-family relationships, discreet enquiries were made to find buyers for the jewels. Because of this, the identity of many of those who purchased individual pieces is known.

Queen Mary, the grandmother of Queen Elizabeth II, acquired a diamond bow clasp. She also secured Maria Pavlovna's favourite pearl and diamond tiara, made in the form of interlaced circles in which pearl and diamond drops were hung. The tiara had been made for the Grand Duchess by a Russian court jeweller in the 1870s, and when Maria left the tiara with Cartier in Paris for cleaning in 1908 the French jeweller was so impressed with the piece that three copies were made.

Queen Mary herself had fifteen emeralds that were known as the 'Cambridge emeralds' because they were added to the royal jewel collection by the Duchess of Cambridge. Mary had the emeralds mounted as drops, creating an alternative to the original pearl decorations on the Russian tiara, and it was worn by her many times.[5] The tiara was eventually left to her grand-daughter in 1953 and Queen Elizabeth continues to wear it on occasions of state, including the Opening of Parliament.

Another tiara, acquired from Cartier by Maria Pavlovna before the First World War – a sapphire and diamond *kokoschnik* with a central sapphire weighing 137 carats – was bought at about the same time by Queen Maria of Romania and worn at her coronation in 1922. The tiara was then passed to her daughter Princess Ileana on her marriage to Archduke Anton of Austria in 1931.[6]

* * *

It is useful to take a look at the financial situations that faced the children of Maria Pavlovna at the beginning of the 1920s, as they were forced to liquidise their remaining assets to varying degrees to safeguard their futures.

Grand Duke Kyril, the eldest of Maria's sons, had shocked his relatives by leading his troops to the Duma, red flag prominently displayed, on the outbreak of the Revolution. His family were the first to leave Russia back in June 1917. His departure had been far more organised, and he had been able to remove some of his more valuable possessions. By the 1920s the family were living relatively comfortably in the South of France, with additional property in Paris and Coburg.

His brother Andrei, on the other hand, took little or nothing of value out of Russia. His partner Mathilde Kschessinska, the former prima ballerina who became Princess Romanovsky-Krassinsky when they married in 1921, described their immediate difficulties in her memoirs:

> The question of money had come up in crucial fashion from the very first day of our life as émigrés. We had left Russia penniless, having lost all we had; all we had left was seven thousand francs in the bank at Monte Carlo. In the beginning we were able to make ends meet by mortgaging the villa. [Andrei] received his share of the inheritance after the death of the Grand Duchess Maria Pavlovna, but the time for selling precious stones was over, and we received a much smaller sum than we expected.[7]

Andrei also entertained hopes of gleaning additional income from estates in Poland, but expectations were dashed when that part of the country was restored in 1922 to the newly established Union of Soviet Socialist Republics.

Mathilde, meanwhile, met up at this time with members of the *Ballet Russes* in Paris and in the South of France, including Serge Diaghilev, Anna Pavlova and Tamara Karsavina. It seemed a logical step from sharing fond memories of the stage to setting up a dance studio in Paris in the hope that it might provide a means of earning a living. The studio turned out to be an outstanding success, and in the mid-1930s the supremely talented Margot Fonteyn joined as a pupil. In 1936, at the age of sixty-four, Mathilde was herself persuaded to take the stage one final time at Covent Garden. She received eighteen curtain calls.

Boris Vladimirovich also escaped from Russia with little of value, although he later had cause to remember that he had opened an account in St Petersburg with the First National City Bank of New York. He was not sure how much was left on deposit, but since it was in a foreign bank he assumed it might be possible to claim all or part of it. On his first visit to New York in the 1920s, Boris asked his private secretary Alexei Pilatsky to contact the bank.[8] They looked into the matter and responded a few days later with the news that the account contained 375,000 roubles, equivalent to $187,500 at the time of his claim. Because of the financial uncertainty of the period, and in view of negotiations going on between the bank and the Soviet authorities, they agreed to let him have ten per cent in part payment.

For Maria's daughter Helen, life had changed beyond recognition. After leaving Athens for a life of temporary exile in 1917, she and her husband Nicholas had moved first to Switzerland and later to France. From palaces and villas, they were now living in apartments and hotels. As Nicholas was a highly-cultured man with a talent for painting, he would eventually make a modest living for his family from his art.

Helen, according to current members of the family, was said to have received the bulk of her mother's jewellery collection. The family maintains that Maria did not fully favour her sons in her will, in part because of Kyril's act of disloyalty during the outbreak of the Revolution, but also because their mother was not particularly enamoured with her sons' choice of partners.

Maria's own ruby collection was given to Helen and later left to Queen Frederika of Greece in Helen's will. A tiara was also gifted by Helen to her daughter Princess Elizabeth of Greece for her wedding, and is now in the possession of Elizabeth's daughter Princess Helene of Habsburg.[9] Elizabeth's children – Count Hans Toerring-Jettenbach and Princess Helene – received, and still possess, Maria's set of blue sapphire jewels. Princess Marina received parts of Maria's white set, now presumably held by the Duchess of Kent, Princess Michael of Kent and Princess Alexandra.

Kyril, Boris and Andrei, on the other hand, almost certainly received the bequest they had been promised – the original allocation of the jewels bought by their father Vladimir.

* * *

The jewels taken from the Vladimir Palace by Albert Stopford were involved in some remarkable adventures. By the time they were safely returned to Maria in post-war France, they had been spirited away from the Vladimir Palace in the dead of night, wrapped in newspaper and stuffed into Gladstone bags, before being smuggled secretly out of Russia and brought to London.

Then, after Maria's death but before the jewels could be distributed or sold off, the collection had been at the centre of an audacious blackmail threat. Before having the jewels valued by Cartier in Paris, it was decided to transfer them to Geneva to escape higher inheritance taxes in London. A courier from the Spanish Embassy in London was engaged to take the items in person, presumably in the diplomatic bag, to Switzerland. On his arrival, however, the courier succumbed to temptation and blackmailed Maria's family into

paying compensation for their safe delivery. When the scandal found its way into the newspapers, the courier was arrested, imprisoned in Spain, and the jewels thankfully returned.

The fate of the sapphire and diamond tiara is just as interesting. The tiara was sold privately in 1920 to Marie of Romania before being passed on to her daughter Ileana on the day of her wedding. But this was just the beginning of its travels, as Ileana explained:

> I lent it to [my mother] to wear at the Jubilee of King George V of England, and she left it in her bank in London because of unsettled conditions at home. After her death I had no small trouble in claiming it, but I got it away from England just before World War II began. I kept it in Austria until 1943 when I smuggled it into Rumania, and there I saved it from the Communists when I left in 1948. It went to Switzerland with me, and then to Argentina, where I pawned it to put money into an unfortunate business that failed.[10]

Ileana later redeemed the tiara before taking it by air over the Andes to America in a small bag wrapped in her nightgown. On arrival at Miami customs she asked if she might open her bag in private. Reluctantly they agreed, and after the customs officer had gingerly touched the central sapphire, which was 'nearly the size of a man's pocket watch', it was decided that customs would have to send it on to Boston 'in bond'.[11]

The tiara and Ileana then travelled to Boston separately. Unable to retrieve the tiara for nearly a fortnight, Ileana finally went to the customs office to pick it up. From there she walked straight up the street to the local post office and mailed it directly to a jeweller in New York for safekeeping. From then on, according to Ileana, it was either treated with great care ('guarded by police') or with abandon ('my son carried it about in the sub-way'), before being sold to an American 'for a sum much below its value'.[12]

Helen also told an intriguing story about her jewels. Having returned to Greece by the time of her inheritance in 1920, she faced another period of turmoil during the next few years in Athens as one government followed another, and successive monarchs took the throne. In 1922 her brother-in-law Constantine was forced to abdicate for a second time, and she and Prince Nicholas, as well as his other brothers, were made to leave once again. Helen and her family moved back to Switzerland, but were unable to take much in the way of valuables with them. It was left to her brother-in-law Prince Christopher to attempt a Stopford-style rescue.

With help from local people Christopher gathered together his own belongings, along with Helen's inherited jewels safely packed in a wooden box, Nicholas's securities and valuables, and Helen's beloved white Persian cat.

Christopher and his tutor arranged for a small rowing boat to be ready for them in Piraeus harbour, and they loaded it up with Helen's wooden box, several cases, and the cat in a basket. They then rowed steadily out to an Italian vessel where they had already booked their passage. But the bobbing movement of the boat set the cat off and its wails drew attention to them as they approached the ship's gangway. Spotting Greek sentries at the top of the gangway, Christopher made to move past them to get to his cabin. 'Instead of stopping when the sentry barred my way I delivered him a tremendous blow in the stomach and before he could recover I sprang past him and rushed into my cabin.'[13] Now considered to be on Italian territory, he was finally safe. His tutor followed at a more sedate pace, bearing the luggage, the jewels, and the cat.

On an overnight stay at a hotel in Brindisi, the cat managed to escape from Christopher and had to be chased out of a neighbour's room by a waiter. Caught and confined, it then wailed loud enough to keep everyone awake on the final rail journey, escaping once again at their destination to hide behind hot water pipes. Dragged out by its tail, the cat was 'now a spitting fury covered in soot'.[14]

Arriving at his sister-in-law's hotel in Switzerland, Christopher was surprised to find Helen more perturbed about the state of her cat, after he had risked his life to deliver a fortune in jewels. The cat had the last word, however, as it took an instant dislike to Sophie of Greece's grey mongrel cat, and the family were left to sort out 'two infuriated balls, one a dirty white, the other grey, whirling in the midst of dust and flying fur'.[15] The cats were eventually separated by well-aimed kicks and a jug of water.

* * *

Maria Pavlovna's family were not the only displaced émigrés forced to offload valuables to make a life for themselves in their new countries. They needed cash not jewels to live on. But by the 1920s it was a buyer's market, and prices were inevitably forced down against the sellers. Maria Pavlovna's family complained as much, but others such as Xenia Alexandrovna, the Tsar's sister, were sadly swindled when her matchless pearls were pawned at this time for £20,000 (c.£599,000 today).[16]

The future security of the émigrés' depended on what they had been able to bring out of Russia with them, or how much others had saved on their behalf. Felix Yusupov, for example, had escaped with enough valuables to keep him and his family in reasonable comfort for many years, initially by raising cash against his treasures and later when he was forced to sell some of the world's most valuable gems. Most of his collection was sold to Cartier in the 1930s, although he retained the magnificent La Pelegrina pearl as long as he could, eventually selling this exquisite jewel in 1953. It came up for auction in the late 1980s, making over $300,000.

The buyers too were changing. Although a few individual gems were taken up by European royals, the world's moneyed wealth, once the prerogative of the Edwardian society of Albert Stopford and his friends, had slowly accumulated in the United States of America. It was no surprise that Cartier's New York office was gradually becoming a crucial link in the transfer of Romanov jewels into rich American hands. Soon the wives and daughters of steel, oil, tin, automobile and banking barons, were vying with Hollywood stars to acquire the latest Russian bauble to come onto the market.

Nancy Leeds, former wife of the tin magnate William Leeds, and one of Stopford's guests at the Savoy before the war, acquired Maria Pavlovna's diadem with the Beauharnais ruby – originally owned by Empress Joséphine de Beauharnais, the first wife of Napoléon Bonaparte – as a wedding present for her son's wife, Princess Xenia. Maria's emeralds were also bought by Cartier and remounted in a diadem for the daughter of John D. Rockefeller. This piece was later acquired by the Woolworth heiress Barbara Hutton. Much later, Richard Burton gave Elizabeth Taylor an emerald and diamond brooch containing some of Maria Pavlovna's emeralds as an engagement present. When they married, he bought her a necklace, also made with Maria's emeralds.[17]

Out of the depths of Stopford's shabby Gladstone bags emerged gems that were destined to adorn the rich and famous for decades – royalty, film stars, entrepreneurs, heiresses and celebrities alike – including Maria's immediate family, two Queens of Great Britain, a Queen of Greece and Queen of Romania, two Duchesses of Kent, Princess Alexandra, Princess Michael of Kent, Princess Helene of Habsburg, Countess Elisabeth (the wife of Count Hans Veit Toerring-Jettenbach), Barbara Hutton and Elizabeth Taylor.

Maria Pavlovna's family recalled visiting Bertie Stopford in his Parisian apartment and being shown the famous Gladstone bags with understandable pride. He later used them to bring a friend's son's clothes through French customs. Stopford naturally could not resist telling his friend that they once contained no less than twenty-five tiaras belonging to Grand Duchess Maria Pavlovna of Russia.

* * *

It is one thing to trace what happened to individual jewels saved by Albert Stopford; it is quite another to estimate the value of his efforts. The list must include, first of all, the jewels distributed among Maria Pavlovna's family in 1920. It should also include the jewels sold in

1920-21 by Helen of Greece to Queen Mary of Great Britain and Queen Marie of Romania, and those left in Helen's will to individuals such as Queen Frederika of Greece.

In addition, there were the other jewels brought out by Stopford that belonged to Serge Obolensky's mother Marie Narishkin and, according to Obolensky, the jewels of other Romanov families.

Rough values can be put on a few individual items. The worth of Grand Duchess Maria's pearl and diamond tiara bought by Queen Mary, and now owned by Queen Elizabeth II, has never been officially reported, but a London newspaper attempted a valuation of Queen Elizabeth's entire jewel collection in 1989 and estimated the tiara's worth at £1,460,000 (c.£2,205,000 today).[18] If the tiara's royal connections are taken into account, some believe its current value might be worth many times that figure.

Maria Pavlovna's sapphire and diamond tiara, bought by Marie of Romania, was valued by her daughter in New York in the 1940s at $80,000 (c.£500,000 today),[19] a figure she felt was significantly under value. The tiara made of rubies, including the magnificent Beauharnais ruby, acquired from Cartier by Maria Pavlovna in 1908 and bought (through Cartier) by Nancy Leeds in 1921, would now be worth over £1 million. Cartier also retains full details of the set of rubies bought by Grand Duke Vladimir for his wife in 1900. It cost him 300,000 French francs at that time.[20]

Finally, there is a clue to the value of the inheritance shared between Kyril, Andrei and Boris in the 1920s in a memorandum from Boris's private secretary Alexei Pilatsky in New York.[21] Boris had received c.$350,000 in the form of emeralds at that time (equivalent to over £2 million in today's value). Pilatsky gave his word that this was the correct figure, as he was handling the Grand Duke's investments. Boris sold the emeralds and invested the money in American stocks under the guidance of the Bankers Trust Company. (It is assumed that both Kyril and Andrei received roughly the same amount as Boris.)

The potential worth of the jewels that belonged to Serge Obolensky's mother and the other Russian émigrés is the final piece of the jigsaw, although it is difficult to quantify. From the time Stopford and his friends at Yalta planned their rescue missions, Stopford and Yusupov became involved in the saving of millions of pounds worth of jewels. Obolensky, however, was in no fit state to assist them. Having gone to the Crimea to recuperate from serious ill health, he then found himself facing personal danger as a suspected White Army officer in an increasingly Red part of the country.[22]

While his wife Catherine Yourievsky remained in Yalta, Obolensky was persuaded to join a White Russian militia in the Tartar Republic organised by an acquaintance, General Peter Wrangel. But after becoming involved in skirmishes in and around Yalta and Sebastopol, Obolensky knew that the task as hopeless. The Red Army was gaining territory throughout the entire area. In a bid to escape capture, he disguised himself and sought refuge in a hospital. Friends then had him moved to Moscow as a 'patient' with a nurse in attendance. Keeping his identity secret, Obolensky took a job in a textile business and arranged to get Catherine out of Yalta to Moscow, where she was able to take a job as a French teacher. The couple eventually joined a trade mission to Kiev in a bid to get out of the country and finally reached the safety of Vienna then Switzerland after three months.

Obolensky's mother, meanwhile, had already escaped to Finland. Her jewels had been secured from Petrograd by Stopford and were now being safely held in a bank in London. Obolensky said that as a child he had been fascinated by his mother's jewellery. Living at Tsarskoe Selo, near the Tsar's Palace, he remembered how his mother looked in her formal court dress, ready to attend one of the grand occasions.

> [She had] whole sets of jewellery, from tiara and ear-rings down to brooches, necklaces and stomachers. … I loved to look at the jewels. I was particularly fascinated by the deep, glowing blue of the sapphires. But I also loved the rubies and emeralds.[23]

After the Revolution, Obolensky was reacquainted with the jewels once again, thanks to the bravery of his friend Bertie Stopford.

> It was strange to see them again, to recall the world of the Court balls, and the glamorous image I retained of mother and father dressing for the Court ceremonies.[24]

The sale of the jewels, piece by piece, enabled Serge's mother to spend the rest of her life in relative comfort.

If one were to add the Obolensky jewels to those of the Grand Duchess Maria Pavlovna, and take account of other Romanov pieces saved by Albert Stopford, it might be possible to gauge their total worth. Obolensky hazarded a guess that the value ran into millions of pounds. The valuation of merely a few of the individual jewels, estimated above, would certainly support this guess. To change the full total into today's sterling, allowing for intervening inflation, the Bank of England's latest estimates suggest that the overall figure should be multiplied by at least twenty times. This equates to a staggering tens of millions of pounds worth of jewels.

D. H. Lawrence's Dream

DURING the 1920s Stopford spent some time away from Paris on the beautiful island of Sicily. The resort of Taormina on the north east of the island had been a regular refuge for the Englishman since the turn of the century and he enjoyed many winters in the sunshine, avoiding the rigours of life in London and Paris. Following his prison sentence, Stopford escaped once again to the peace and quiet of his villa Casa Vinciguerra, known locally as Casa Stopford, where he happily tended an old monastery garden full of roses close to the Cappuccini Convent, and another garden rising in terraces above the church of S. Giuseppe. The villa was only a stone's throw from one of the most beautiful town squares on the island, the Piazza Nove Aprile in Taormina, with its magnificent views over the sea.[1]

Although more a haven for tourists these days, Taormina was and still is a small village atop a spectacular promontory, and it is easy to see what attracted Stopford to the town in the first place. Like Capri it was a magnet for a select group of ex-patriates, including a few upper-class English people who found the sunshine and cost of living to their liking, some European literary figures seeking inspiration and solitude, and a number of individuals desperate, for their own reasons, to escape prejudice and intolerance. For Stopford, Taormina was a welcome retreat from the strict confines of Edwardian society and it was hardly surprising that such a gregarious character would become a familiar and accepted member of the small community.

As early as 1902 the intrepid traveller Gertrude Bell ran into Stopford during a short visit on her way to the Middle East. Walking with some companions up behind the piazza, Getrude had by chance chosen his garden wall as a spot from which to take a photograph. Stopford was in the garden replanting an almond tree and invited Gertrude's party in for a chat. He showed them around the terraces and handed out small bunches of violets as they left.[2]

According to Taormina's historical records, Stopford's offerings of flowers from his garden hit a high spot when King Edward VII visited the town in 1906, following in the footsteps of other royals such as Kaiser Wilhelm and the King of Siam. It was said that Edward spent time with Stopford at his villa, and from his garden he offered the king some dark crimson tea-roses with a coppery centre and a strong fragrance. The roses, called 'Albert Stopford',[3] were propagated in 1898 by the well-known French horticulturalist Gilbert Nabonnard who often called his new creations after his clients.

There were other visitors of note to the island, including the writer D. H. Lawrence and his wife Frieda who spent time there between 1920 and 1922. Although vaguely aware of some scandal involving Stopford in London, they found him to be a pleasant lunch companion and 'really very nice'.[4] The Lawrences rented a beautiful, isolated house, the Fontana Vecchia, facing the Ionian sea on the outskirts of Taormina. It was there that Lawrence wrote *The Lost Girl* and *Mr Noon*, parts of *Birds, Beasts and Flowers* and *Aaron's Rod*, as well as the beginning of *Sea and Sardinia*.

The Lawrences occasionally invited Stopford to dine at Fontana Vecchia, although one of Lawrence's last letters to Stopford contained an apology for having had to cancel at short notice:

> ... do please forgive me if I ask you to let me off the Sunday luncheon I planned. I am sorry – but all is just a whirl here. ... We must leave for Palermo on Monday.[5]

As a memento of their friendship, Lawrence sent Stopford a signed copy of *The Rainbow*, 'the only copy of this edition which I have signed'.[6] He also sent a photograph of them together, taken by a local friend with Stopford's camera.

Stopford clearly left his mark on Lawrence, for the author wrote to a friend that when he was in Sicily he felt

> ... as if one had lived there for a hundred thousand years. What it is that is so familiar I don't know. You remember Stopford said Sicily had been waiting for me for about 2000 years: must be the sense of that long wait. Not that Sicily waited for me alone:
>> She waits for each other
>> She waits for all men born. [Swinburne][7]

Oscar Wilde was also a visitor to the island, although there is no evidence to suggest that the paths of Wilde and Stopford ever crossed – in Taormina, Paris or in London – despite the fact that they moved in some of the same circles. Stopford's friend Lady Gladys de Grey, for example, had known Wilde for many years.

Authors like Tennessee Williams and Truman Capote were also drawn to Sicily, renting D. H. Lawrence's villa in Taormina. Hollywood was also not far behind, and it is known that Greta Garbo stayed briefly on the island at the house of the famous nutritionist and self-help author Gayelord Hauser.

In his later years on the island, Stopford liked to dine out on his adventures in Tsarist Russia and his connections with the likes of Edward VII and George V. In company he was known to produce a 'heavy cigarette case of gold, studded with brilliants, set in the shape of an imperial crown'.[8] He said it had been given to him by Tsar Nicholas II.

Stopford also loved to spend hours on the beach where he clearly held forth to friends and acquaintances. One local writer described him as

> ... tall and straight as a plank, with a salt and pepper tiny moustache, a monocle hanging on his always red waistcoat, when he came to spend the whole winter in Taormina. ... He was Milord to everybody in Taormina, a *monument to extravagance* and generosity, loved by everybody.[9]

It was said that the poorer townsfolk, aware of his reputation for generosity, would attempt to shine his shoes or guide his walk so that he would not stumble on his regular strolls through the streets. But Stopford was known to be a genuinely kind man and enjoyed giving out small gifts, especially during Easter, when he piled up small pieces of furniture and artefacts outside his house for anyone to take.

> A small crowd of needy gathered on the spot and while the bells tolled joyously the *Gloria*, all were able to put their hands on a painting, a chair, a chandelier, a bunch of silver cutlery.[10]

At times of stress, as we have seen, Stopford had a habit of bringing out his tarot cards to see what the future might bring. He had done so on a number of occasions in Russia and this habit continued into later life. In Sicily D. H. Lawrence witnessed his friend's reliance on the turn of the cards many times, and in 1922 Lawrence wrote to a friend from New Mexico about a dream he had experienced. In his dream Albert Stopford had paid a visit, to warn him that he had read in the cards that something terrible – perhaps another war – was looming in the near future.[11]

Once again, the cards had spoken.

CHAPTER SIXTEEN

A Communal Grave

ONE of Albert Stopford's main concerns after leaving jail in 1919 was to ensure the safe delivery of the jewels to their rightful owners. This had now been achieved. And with the passing of his friends Gladys de Grey and Maria Pavlovna, it must have felt like the end of an era. The grand parties once graced by the upper classes were now few and far between, and in his self-imposed exile to Paris he faced a more restricted social horizon, based around work and the occasional visit to the theatre or art exhibition. Perhaps only in his seasonal escapes to Taormina did Stopford relive some of his glory days and feel some sense of freedom from his recent fall from grace.

There was still the occasional lunch or dinner to look forward to, sometimes in his apartment, sometimes out with friends. Of those from London, only Juliet Duff, Mrs Hwfa Williams, Georgina Buchanan, Nellie Melba and the Duchess of Sutherland continued to associate with him, and even then usually in Paris. Contacts in England were now limited to Stopford's solicitor, his bank, a literary agent and, rather intriguingly, two inspectors from Scotland Yard.

Juliet Duff was an early visitor to his apartment in the Palais Royal, and Mrs Hwfa Williams would often pop round when staying in her Parisian residence. Her admiration for Stopford's dancing never diminished. The family of Maria Pavlovna – particularly Helen, Andrei and Mathilde – were also more than happy to relive old times whenever they were in the capital, often bringing news of Dmitri Pavlovich whom they met from time to time.

Stopford was similarly delighted to keep up with friends from the Diaghilev ballet. When Anna Pavlova was performing in Paris, he wrote in a letter to a friend that she 'danced beautifully on Saturday. ... I later had lunch with her'.[1] He also dined with Nellie Melba a few days before her final departure from Europe, an occasion he recorded with a touch of nostalgia: 'I first met her over dinner in 1888 with the Duc d'Orléans, who was then living in London.'[2]

The names of a few loyal friends in London were written in bold letters in Stopford's address book. This was among a number of precious items belonging to Albert Stopford that were kept by his namesake John, the young man of the Russian Armoured Car Division who left Petrograd within a day of Albert in 1917. Other mementoes still in the possession of John's family include a silver cigarette box engraved with 'A. S.', a Cartier clock with an enamel face, and an invitation to Albert's funeral in Paris in 1939.[3]

The two men may have been in touch during the mid-1920s when Albert discovered that John was in the oil business and based in Ploesti, Romania, not far from where he had fought eight or nine years before. It is not known if they actually met up, but Albert did enquire about the precise times the diplomatic bag was due to leave Paris for Romania.

Wishing to remain involved with anything associated with Russia, Stopford also became a willing contact for refugees from the Soviet regime. There were many displaced and destitute souls during the 1920s and '30s, some seeking pre-war wealth in Western banks, others needing an escape route to the West. But sadly, where money called, crooks were often not far behind.

Stopford had a close friend called Jean Panayotti, a Greek subject born in Russia. He had been told of a Russian refugee family, Nestor and Eudoxia Fillia and their daughter Ada, who were desperate to get to Switzerland where they had deposited a considerable sum of money in the Federal Bank of Geneva. Any individual who could help them to escape would be well rewarded. A plot was devised that would link the family's escape from Russia with the possible capture of a former OGPU agent in the Soviet intelligence service, George Agebakov, also known as Nerses Ovsepian. The latter had defected to Britain in 1930 and had already published his memoirs, much to the disquiet of his former Soviet employers in the Kremlin.

Stopford entered into the plot with characteristic enthusiasm, encouraging parallel talks in Bucharest, and shuttling between Paris and Brussels in an effort to bring the affair to a successful conclusion. Despite his efforts, George Agebakov evaded these complex attempt by the Soviets to capture him and was to live a few more years in Paris before finally disappearing under suspicious circumstances in 1938. There seems little doubt, however, that the OGPU had finally caught up with the agent.

* * *

There is no evidence that Stopford benefited significantly from the jewels he had rescued. His lifestyle in Paris during this time showed little relative affluence and he was more often the guest than the host at lunch or dinner. His correspondence also strongly suggests that he was earning his own living by necessity, in order to supplement a regular quarterly transfer from Lloyds Bank on the Strand in central London.

Stopford was now firmly re-established in the world of antiques, and the business that had been so profitable for him in the past. But reflecting the enormous changes brought about by the war, both in society and in the global economy, his focus had switched from jewellery to English furniture and silverware.

His clients were now wealthy businessmen visiting Paris, mostly from America. Stopford acted as a middle-man between antique dealers and clients out to furnish their new homes in the French capital, or high-spending tycoons who wanted to create valuable collections with their newly-acquired wealth.

Ralph Strassburger and his wife May from Pennsylvania were typical clients.[4] Strassburger had served in the United States Navy and diplomatic corps, while May was heiress to the Singer sewing-machine company. In addition to their home in Pennsylvania, the couple owned an apartment in Paris, a farm near Deauville and property in Chantilly. They were keen to build a collection of English furniture and sterling silver.

Stopford liked to impress the Strassburgers with his society connections. The Duc d'Orleans or the Duc de Valencay were names that he could casually drop into the conversation, but the Strassburgers were particularly impressed when they were introduced in person to Princess Helen and Prince Nicholas of Greece, and Grand Duke Andrei Vladimirovich and his wife Princess Romanovsky-Krassinsky. And in 1924, with the newspapers full of George V's sudden illness and the efforts of his doctor Sir Francis Laking to contain the infection, Stopford did not fail to mention that Laking was also his family's doctor.

Stopford's job was to search out objects for the Strassburgers in Paris and later, as his infamy faded, in London. Sometimes he attended auctions and special exhibitions on the Strassburger's behalf, occasionally persuading dealers to provide special pieces on approval. When the antiques were destined for the couple's apartment in Paris, Stopford was pleased to supervise their installation in person.

As their business relationship grew, Stopford undertook other chores on their behalf, such as arranging for 'the best polisher in London'[5] to do work for them in Paris. He even brought their son's clothes through customs from London in one of the famous Gladstone bags, and sent his valet – referred to as his man, George – round to the son's apartment to deliver them. Whether George was a valet or a male companion is, on the face of it, hard to judge. But the way George organised parts of Stopford's life, and his dealings on behalf of his clients, strongly suggests a more equal partnership.

By the late 1920s Stopford felt able to visit London more often, buying the cheapest rail ticket across the Channel and staying perhaps three or four days. He would often meet Lady Juliet for lunch, visit the opera or ballet, talk to a few dealers with specific purchases in mind, and return with photographs of recommended pieces for his clients in Paris. He usually stayed at the Grosvenor Hotel and dined at the Savoy, no doubt at his clients' expense.

Stopford met the photographer and artist Cecil Beaton in London at this time, and managed to persuade Beaton on a visit to Paris to take pictures of him in his Palais Royal apartment.[6]

All in all, Stopford seemed to be keeping his head above water during the 1920s, but it was not to last. As the boom and bust of the terrible 1929-30 Depression began to bite into his clients' wallets, the level of his own income began to suffer. His health, as he moved into his seventies, was also a matter of real concern. In the autumn of 1930 what he described to his friends as a 'wicked heart attack' affected him very badly: 'I thought I was going for good.'[7]

Stopford recovered his health for a time, but his finances were not so robust. The stock market crash of 1929 left currency devaluations and higher interest rates in its wake, and the loss of value of the French franc reduced the amount of regular income Stopford received from his London bank. When the Bank of France, the landlord of his section of the Palais Royal apartments, increased his rent, Stopford was plunged into a crisis.

This led to an immediate *cri de coeur* to the Strassburgers. His correspondence with them at this time reveals that, in addition to paying for his business services, they had also been subsidising his rent:

> ... it was you with Strass who made that generous gift about my rent. ... Since then French law has increased all rents – last October and again this quarter – and, instead of 3,500 francs a quarter the rent now amounts to 4,160 francs. ...
>
> I expect no money before July 22 (my solicitor writes) and I hear that if I don't pay the full amount the Banque de France may turn me out. So I have asked Strass if I may have this addition to the rent that you and he so kindly pay.[8]

Ralph Strassburger proved to be a generous man, and Stopford was quick to acknowledge his overwhelming relief to his wife May:

> This morning a letter and cheque from Strass. How good and kind and generous. If you knew the relief it was to me! I will sleep hours tonight, please God. ... But for you I wouldn't be here.[9]

Throughout the 1930s the decline in Stopford's work, coupled with a marked deterioration in his health, took its toll on his income. He was now in his mid-seventies and clearly living from hand to mouth. A sudden stop in his regular money transfer from the Strassburgers in 1937 finally brought home to Stopford what a precarious situation he was in. He wrote to May in a panic:

> As you know for years Strass has most generously paid the rent for my apartment. On Thursday morning Lloyds bank told me they had no instructions from him to do so. I found myself with the rent to pay and no money to pay it. If I had known before I might have taken some precaution.
>
> It is 26 years that I have lived here, and it is terrible to have to leave at my age – 77 years past – especially as I hardly ever go out anyhow. We will see what will happen.
>
> If ever you find yourself near this part of Paris, do come in. I am here every afternoon.[10]

In yet another letter of thinly-veiled complaint he wrote, 'things are so bad that after today I do not know what to do – what I ask for is to be able to live and eat.'[11]

It is known that Stopford managed to keep his apartment, so the Strassburgers must have bailed him out. But he was now a shadow of the man he used to be, becoming increasingly infirm and living on past memories. His social circle had now contracted to a few close friends, and when he drew up his will, with the help of his solicitor in London,[12] Stopford left his entire estate to George, identified in his will and address book as Jorge Enrico Medina, a Colombian from Bogota.

The end came in February 1939, seven months before the outbreak of the Second World War. Albert Henry Stopford died leaving little more than £900 in his estate, a relatively modest amount in comparison to the millions of pounds worth of fabulous treasures he had bravely smuggled out of the chaos of the Russian Revolution.

When Stopford made arrangements for his burial at Bagneux Cemetery on the outskirts of Paris,[13] there was no agreement about the future upkeep of the grave. He was finally laid to rest in February 1939 in plot 571, burial place no. 1, in the 2nd row of the 39th division.[14] Unlike Oscar Wilde, however, buried in the same cemetery nearly forty years before him, Stopford had no friends to rescue his body from final humiliation. Thirty years after his death, with no funds in place for the upkeep of the plot, the body of Albert Henry Stopford was transferred to a communal grave.

EPILOGUE

'A Monument to Extravagance'

ALBERT STOPFORD left little trace of himself in Paris where he had lived on a permanent basis for almost twenty years until his death. It was an anonymous ending for one so used to being in the centre of his own social circle.

The Edwardian world in which Bertie Stopford had lived life to the full had vanished. The monarchical society of his youth had been shattered by a terrible war. Of the nine kings, seven queens and five heir-apparents of European dynasties who attended King Edward VII's funeral in 1910, only a handful of constitutional monarchs remained. And with this shift in power came another shift – from inherited wealth to a more widespread capitalist-based economy. The society of Stopford's friends had gone forever, and those that survived were now living in a very different age, where talent would replace privilege, and wealth would no longer accumulate, as if by right, in the hands of the few.

The extravagance enjoyed in European capitals right up to the First World War had fizzled out. The spending power of royalty in the glittering premises of Fabergé and Cartier was replaced after the war by the growing wealth of New World business.

Stopford's Russian friends, in the aftermath of the Revolution, were perhaps simply relieved to be facing this new era with their lives. Given the brutal conclusion to Tsar Nicholas's reign, many members of the Tsarist court had been killed or forced into exile. Families were scattered across the world, arriving ill-prepared in foreign lands with little more than the clothes on their backs or precious belongings stuffed into bags and pockets. No longer in receipt of income from the state, many would now earn their own living. Of the Romanovs who escaped from their homeland, one became a champagne salesman, another an interior decorator, one a local mayor in Florida, two joined the banking industry, and while one ended up working for British Intelligence, another joined the Central Intelligence Agency in America.

Looking back on the life of Albert Stopford during the first two decades of the twentieth century, it is easy to detect a flaw or two, or at least, as Serge Obolensky once said, 'a moment's weakness' after the dark days of the Russian Revolution. When Stopford returned to London from Petrograd in October 1917 he was at the end of his tether. Having endured hunger, extreme cold, ill-health and indiscriminate gun-fire in Petrograd, he faced untold risk to bring jewels that did not belong to him out of a country beset with unimaginable violence. The fear that must have gripped him as he passed through Russian customs for the last time may be difficult to comprehend, but it was real enough.

It is perhaps easier to understand Stopford's sense of relief as he walked the relatively peaceful streets of London. The disgrace that befell him within months of his return stemmed from his sexual inclinations and the ease with which these could be satisfied in a country still at war. Obolensky maintained that Stopford had 'lost his bearings with the ending of the tension he had lived under'.[1] But whether he was indeed part of a blackmail ring, as he was accused of 'in a pitiless blaze of tabloid publicity',[2] remains unproven. That he persuaded, if not pressurised, at least one guardsman absent without leave to have a sexual relationship with him, can hardly be denied.

Whatever the truth behind the accusations, many of his erstwhile friends judged him on the strength of the trial's publicity, and he left jail, and London, with his former life in tatters.

Ever resourceful, however, Stopford returned to Paris and to his antiques business for much-needed income to tide him over. But now that Lady Gladys and 'his Grand Duchess' Maria Pavlovna had gone, he became more circumspect about the need for a wide social circle. His later years would be spent in the company of George with the occasional visits of a few loyal friends who appreciated his colossal strengths and unerring acts of kindness.

Serge Obolensky was one such friend. Witnessing the incipient deterioration in Stopford's health on their last meeting in the Crimea, he summed up Bertie Stopford as 'an unfailing friend to all of us in any hour of need',[3] a sentiment echoed by others, who took him as he was – 'a *monument to extravagance and generosity*, loved by everybody'.[4]

APPENDIX

ALBERT Stopford would no doubt have relished one final ripple in the story of Grand Duchess Maria Pavlovna and the fortunes of her family after the Revolution.

A brief mention of Albert Stopford in my earlier book, *The Lost Fortune of the Tsars*,[1] and preliminary inquiries about him for this publication, prompted a letter from a reader in America who wondered whether a memorandum written by an uncle, who had a previous connection with a Romanov grand duke, would be of interest. The memorandum turned out to be a sixty-page document written by Alexei Edmundovich Pilatsky, who had been secretary to Boris Vladimirovich in New York in the 1920s.[2]

Pilatsky's memorandum is not dissimilar to many written by White Russians and deals with his education in Tsarskoe Selo and at Moscow University, his appointment in the Ministry of Transport, and his involvement with General Lavr Kornilov, and later with General Anton Deniken at White Army headquarters. Pilatsky eventually escaped from Russia to Paris through the Crimea, and travelled on from there to the United States and New York.

Boris Vladimirovich and his wife Zinaida arrived in New York aboard the *Bremen* in 1926, and Pilatsky was employed by the Grand Duke as his secretary. It was Pilatsky who confirmed that the funds Boris originally placed in the St Petersburg branch of the First National City Bank of New York before the Revolution would still be available to him.[3]

Pilatsky's memorandum also described the sharing out of Grand Duchess Maria's jewels among her four children, and mentioned an account in the 'something and Midland' bank in London.

Being reasonably familiar with London's financial centre, I recognised this as the London Joint City and Midland Bank, one of the original smaller banks that merged to become the Midland Bank in 1923 and is now part of the HSBC Group. I asked the archivist at the bank whether an account had ever been set up in the name of Maria or Boris Vladimirovich. After a few weeks the bank rang to say that no account had been opened in these names, but an account in the name of Grand Duke Andrei Vladimirovich had been set up in June 1918.

My first instinct was to assume that the account had something to do with the activities of Albert Stopford and his connection with the British Embassy and Grand Duchess Maria's family. But in June 1918 Stopford was in Wormwood Scrubs, and Maria, along with Boris and Andrei, were still in the Caucasus.

The bank later confirmed that this was an unclaimed account and had never been used. On further investigation it was revealed that it had been opened on 3 June 1918, and an original sum of £5000 (worth c.£106,000 today) had been deposited by an individual named as H. A. Farran Leech [Hugh Ausdell Farran Leech].

From an examination of the account in London,[4] H. A. Farran Leech was identified simply as 'British Embassy, Petrograd'. It was also revealed that Leech also had an account at the same bank, and that he received regular sums of money from the Postmaster General, the Government's paying agent and in turn paid out individual sums. On 1 June 1918, £428,571 was paid into Leech's account (equivalent to c.£9,000,000 today) from the Postmaster General. Two days later Leech credited Andrei's account with the £5000.

It is known that Andrei was not in London during the years immediately after leaving Russia in 1920, as confirmed in one of Maria Pavlovna's last letters.[5] And although Andrei and his wife Mathilde did visit London in the late 1920s, no attempt was made to use the account. As it continued to remain untouched after Andrei's death in October 1956, it can be inferred that he did not know of its existence.

It is to Leech that we must look for an explanation, and to his activities at the British Embassy in Petrograd in the years following the Revolution. George Buchanan had left Petrograd by January 1918 and his Counsellor, Francis Lindley, was now in charge. Lindley was assisted by Colonel Keyes as his political and financial agent. Following the eight months of the Provisional Government under Lvov and Kerensky, and the final victory of the Bolsheviks under Lenin, the British Embassy was having to cope with the new Bolshevik regime and continuing German pressure on the Eastern Front. Colonel Keyes had been appointed chairman of the Anglo-Russian Commission to deal with propaganda and the provision of support to the White Russian armies in the south of the country.

With hindsight, the diplomatic and commercial worlds of the Allied governments failed to understand the full implication of Revolution in March 1917. It was still hoped that business might continue with the new regimes – first the Provisional Government, and then the Bolsheviks – and that it was essential to move into an advantageous relationship ahead of Germany. But British, French, and even American bankers and industrialists all misread the prospects. While this was ongoing, members of the deposed and exiled Romanov family were slowly coming to terms with their own plight and were now anxious to save whatever wealth they could.

In such a climate Farran Leech's financial acumen and local contacts blossomed. He had lived in Russia for a number of years and was married to a Russian girl. As the war continued he became increasingly involved in spying for the Secret Intelligence Service, although he was ostensibly running a financial company with a friend. His company – a commission agency, charging for financial advice in both shares and foreign exchange – provided an obvious channel through which the Embassy could finance British propaganda in Russian newspapers and magazines, without appearing to be directly involved.[6] Leech was eventually appointed head of the British Propaganda Bureau known as the 'Cosmos Agency', under the control of Colonel Keyes, and was given his own room in the Embassy. This was the very Bureau Albert Stopford was seeking to join prior to his arrest in London.

The propaganda activity alone during this time explains why so much British Government money passed through Leech's London account at the London Joint City and Midland Bank. The Embassy would be more likely to channel funds through an agent such as Leech than become directly involved in any actions against the new Russian government, especially after the Bolsheviks took control.

Leech also took on other covert activities, from an audacious attempt to take over the top five Russian banks, if only to thwart the Germans, to a bid to switch sterling into roubles for the various needs of the Embassy.[7] These so-called 'Russian bank schemes' involved Leech working with local Russian financiers to buy up shares (and directorships) in specified local banks. Sterling would then be banked in London in a direct swap for roubles in Russia to finance these takeovers. Faced with Bolshevik ruthlessness, wealthy Russians were desperate to get as much of their money abroad as possible, and individuals readily offered roubles in exchange for accounts in Stockholm, Geneva, Paris and London.

With the political atmosphere so volatile, the opportunity for fraudulent schemes was attractive, but the dangers just as prevalent. As Leech himself later said, he was undertaking financial tasks for the Embassy 'which compelled me to run great personal risks day and night'.[8] The result of these various, sometimes nefarious, financial dealings was a stream of money moving in and out of what the Foreign Office came to describe as 'the Leech account' at the London Joint City and Midland Bank.

But under which category of Leech's activities did Andrei Vladimirovich's untouched account represent? Was he in some way involved with one of these bank schemes by offering roubles in return for an account outside Russia; or was Leech simply helping Andrei to get whatever rouble wealth he had out of the country? As there is no evidence that Andrei was ever involved in these or any banking affairs, a straight swap of roubles for sterling seems by far the best explanation.

It leaves one tantalising question. Why did Leech not inform Andrei of what he had done on his behalf? The Grand Duke would surely have been grateful for access to this money when financial pressures forced him to remortgage his property in Cap d'Ail in the 1920s. It may, however, have been wiser not to alert anyone to the existence of such an account when claims of non-payment arising from some of the deals through the Leech account began to surface in London's High Court in the autumn of 1920.[9]

International banks are now far more active in their efforts to establish claimants and HSBC was keen to find out who the current claimants might be. The answer was not straightforward. Andrei and Mathilde were both deceased and their only son died when young. No other direct descendants existed.

It was at this point that Count Hans Veit Toerring-Jettenbach in Munich, a cousin of the Duke of Kent, Prince Michael of Kent and Princess Alexandra, who had already provided me with considerable guidance in identifying the Stopford jewels, came to the rescue by providing a genealogical family tree of Maria Pavlovna's descendants. The immediate claimants to the London account were the descendants of Andre's two brothers and sister, and in the intervening years since the account was opened it was found that there were twenty-nine eligible descendants scattered across Europe and North America.

During the same period the account had attracted interest. The resultant negotiations between descendants and the bank were soon completed and each individual has now received his or her appropriate share. One instinctively feels that Albert Stopford would have approved.

NOTES TO CHAPTERS

NOTES TO CHAPTER ONE

1. Lady Constance Gladys de Grey (Constance Gwladys Herbert) married the Earl of Lonsdale in 1878 and became the Countess of Lonsdale. After his death in 1882 she married Lord de Grey in 1885 (see note 3 below). Known also as Lady Ripon, Marchioness of Ripon, and the Countess de Grey.
2. Friends of Edward, Prince of Wales were named 'The Marlborough House Set' after his London residence, the centre of their social scene.
3. Lord de Grey (Frederick Oliver Robinson), became 4th Earl de Grey, 3rd Earl of Ripon and 2nd Marquess of Ripon in 1900. Known as Lord Ripon.
4. Charles Neilson Gattey: *Queens of Song* (1979).
5. Nellie Melba: *Melodies and Memories* (1926).
6. H. Montgomery Hyde: *Oscar Wilde* (1976).
7. *The Tatler*, 26 March 1902.
8. Hyde (1976): *ibid*.
9. E. F. Benson: *As We Were* (1930).
10. *The Observer*, 30 June 1929.
11. Richard Buckle: *Diaghilev* (1979).
12. Gabriel Astruc Papers: Dance Division, New York Public Library for the Performing Arts, Lincoln Center, New York.
13. Article by Charles Neilson Gattey: 'Lady de Grey and the Garden's Golden Age', Royal Opera House Archives (Spring 1992).

14. *The Times*, 27 June 1911; *Dancing Times*, June 1971.
15. Tamara Karsavina: *Theatre Street* (1930).
16. *Ibid.*
17. *Ibid.*
18. *Ibid.*
19. Diana Cooper: *The Rainbow Comes and Goes* (1959).
20. M. E. Reynolds: *Memories of John Galsworthy* (1936).
21. Gattey (1992): *ibid.*
22. Mrs Hwfa Williams: *It Was Such Fun* (1935).
23. Serge Obolensky: *One Man in his Time* (1960), p. 87.
24. Obolensky (1960): *ibid.*

CHAPTER TWO

1. See *Burke's Peerage*, *Debrett's* and Crawford's Clerical Register, Royal Kalendar, Lambeth Palace Library Archives.
2. 'A Short Guide to the Church of St Mary the Virgin, Titchmarsh' (1998).
3. 'Titchmarsh', Northampton Record Office.
4. Births, Marriages, Deaths Certificates, Family Records Centre, Myddleton Street, London.
5. Correspondence between Francis Stopford and Canon Luckock, 18 August 1912 [328p/23/2], Northampton Record Office.
6. Helen Belgion: *Titchmarsh Past and Present* (1979).
7. Francis Stopford and Luckock, 2 April 1912 [328p/23/1].

8. Francis Stopford and Luckock, 18 August 1912 [328p/23/2].
9. *ibid.*
10. United Kingdom Censuses for 1871, 1881 and 1891.

CHAPTER THREE

1. United Kingdom Censuses for 1881 and 1891.
2. 'The Court Circular', *The Times*, 26 June 1886.
3. See chapter 12, note 21.
4. *The Times*, 7 October 1901.
5. *New York Times*, 31 Jan. 1905.
6. *NY Times*, 1 Feb. 1905.
7. *NY Times*, 11 May 1913.
8. Geza von Habsburg and Avon Solodkoff: *Fabergé: Court Jeweller to the Tsar* (1979).
9. Fabergé accounts, London branch, 1900s, archives of Wartski, jewellers, 14 Grafton Street, London.
10. Fabergé accounts (1900s): *ibid.*
11. Henry C. Bainbridge: *Peter Carl Fabergé* (1966).
12. Fabergé accounts (1900s): *ibid.*
13. Hans Nadelhoffer: *Cartier: Jewelers Extraordinary* (1984); Julie Rudoe: *Cartier: 1900-1939* (1997).
14. Nadelhoffer (1984): *ibid.*
15. *Ibid.*
16. Nadelhoffer (1984): *ibid.*; Geza von Habsburg: *Fabergé-Cartier, Rivalen am Zarenhof* (Munich 2003). Contributors include Geza von Habsburg, Johan George Prince von Habsburg, Betty Jais [Cartier], Tatiana Fabergé, Alain Cartier

and Alexander von Soldkoff; volume published to accompany 'Cartier Fabergé' Exhibition in Munich, 2003-04.

17. *The Times*, 18 November 1913.
18. Last Will and Testament of Rev. Frederick Manners Stopford, Myddleton Street, London.

CHAPTER FOUR

1. State Archives of the Russian Federation: Grand Duchess Maria Pavlovna Sr., Fond 655, Inventory 1, File 2149.
2. State Archives of the Russian Federation: *ibid.*, letter dated 16 October 1912.
3. *Ibid.*, letter dated 19 November 1912.
4. *Ibid.*
5. *Ibid.*, letter dated 26 November 1912.
6. *Ibid.*
7. *Ibid.*
8. *Ibid.*
9. On 28 December 1908 Messina in Sicily suffered a devastating earthquake.
10. State Archives of the Russian Federation: *ibid.*, letter dated 26 November 1912.

CHAPTER FIVE

1. Christopher Dobson: *Prince Felix Yusupov* (1989). I have also benefited from a private memorandum written by Gretchen Haskin which she allowed me to see.
2. Archivist, University College, Oxford.
3. Prince Felix Youssoupoff: *Lost Splendour* (1953).
4. Serge Obolensky: *One Man in his Time* (1960), p. 86.
5. Private memoir written by Eric Hamilton, University College Archives, Oxford.
6. *Ibid.*
7. *Ibid.*
8. *Ibid.*

9. *Ibid.*
10. *Ibid.*
11. *Ibid.*
12. Youssoupoff (1953): *ibid.*
13. *Ibid.*
14. Juliet Nicholson: *The Perfect Summer: England 1911, Just before the Storm* (2007).
15. Mrs Hwfa Williams: *It Was Such Fun* (1935).
16. Youssoupoff (1953): *ibid.*
17. *Ibid.*
18. Obolensky (1960): *ibid.*, p. 86.
19. Williams (1935): *ibid.*
20. *Ibid.*
21. Youssoupoff (1953): *ibid.*
22. *Ibid.*
23. *Ibid.*
24. *Ibid.*
25. Obolensky (1960): *ibid.*, p. 88.
26. *Ibid.*, p. 110.
27. *Ibid.*, p. 109.
28. Youssoupoff (1953): *ibid.*
29. *Ibid.*
30. *Ibid.*
31. *Ibid.*

CHAPTER SIX

1. Nellie Melba: *Melodies and Memories* (1926).
2. Princess Marie Louise: *My Memories of Six Reigns* (1979).
3. *Ibid.*
4. Barbara Tuchman: *The Guns of August – August 1914* (1962).
5. Anonymous (Albert Henry Stopford): *The Russian Diary of an Englishman: Petrograd 1915-1917* (1919) (from 6 June 1917), p. 163.
6. Michael Harmer: *The Forgotten Hospital* (1982); Wilfred Blunt: *Lady Muriel* (1962); Lady Muriel Paget's papers, Leeds University (Brotherton) Archives.

CHAPTER SEVEN

1. Anonymous (Albert Henry Stopford): *Diary* (1919).

2. *Diary* (21 July 1915), p. 11.
3. *Diary* (3 Sept. 1915), p. 21.
4. *Diary* (22 Aug. 1915), pp. 16-17).
5. *Diary* (1 Sept. 1915), p. 20.
6. *Diary* (2 Oct. 1915), p. 26.
7. *Diary* (3 Oct. 1915), p. 28.
8. *Diary* (15 Nov. 1915), p. 34.
9. *Ibid.*, p. 35.
10. *Diary* (24 May 1916), p. 61.
11. *Diary* (22 Aug. 1915), p. 18.
12. *Diary* (5 Sept. 1915), p. 21.
13. *Ibid.*
14. *Ibid.*, pp. 21-22.
15. *Ibid.*, p. 22.
16. *Diary* (21 Jan. 1916), p. 43.
17. *Diary* (5 Feb. 1916), p. 44.
18. *Diary* (9 Feb. 1916), p. 45.
19. *Ibid.*
20. *Ibid.*
21. *Ibid.*, p. 46.
22. *Diary* (13 Feb. 1916), p. 50.
23. *Ibid.*, p. 47.
24. *Ibid.*, p. 48.
25. *Ibid.*
26. *Ibid.*, p. 50.
27. *Ibid.*, p. 49.
28. *Ibid.*, p. 50.

CHAPTER EIGHT

1. Anonymous (Albert Henry Stopford): *Diary* (1919) (from 28 August 1915), p. 19.
2. *Ibid.*
3. Richard Pipes: *The Russian Revolution 1899-1919* (1990).
4. From *S. Tsarem* by Vladimir Voeikov, quoted in Pipes (1990).
5. Pipes (1990): *ibid.*
6. Edvard Radzinsky: *The Rasputin File* (2000).
7. *Diary* (19 Dec. 1916), p. 73.
8. *Diary* (22 Dec. 1916), p. 74.
9. *Diary* (31 Dec. 1916), p. 75.
10. *Ibid.*, pp. 77-78.
11. *Diary* (Appendix I, Petition), pp. 213-14.
12. *Diary* (2 Jan. 1917), p. 83.
13. *Diary* (6 Jan. 1917), p. 89.
14. *Diary* (2 Jan. 1917), p. 83.
15. *Ibid.*, pp. 83-87.

16. *Diary* (Appendix III, Police Report), pp. 218-22.
17. *Diary* (2 Jan. 1917), p. 86.
18. *Ibid.*, p. 86; (Appendix III, Police Report), p. 220.
19. *Ibid.*
20. *Ibid.*, p. 87.
21. *Ibid.*
22. Prince Felix Youssoupoff: *Lost Splendour* (1953).
23. *Diary* (2 Jan. 1917), p. 87.
24. Radzinsky (2000): *ibid.*
25. *Ibid.*
26. *Ibid.*
27. *Ibid.*
28. Edvard Radzinsky: *The Rasputin File* (2000).
29. Marie, Grand Duchess of Russia: *Education of a Princess* (1931).
30. BBC Two, Timewatch documentary, 'Who Killed Rasputin?', 1 October 2004; Andrew Cook: *To Kill Rasputin: The Life and Death of Grigori Rasputin* (2005). See also http://en.wikipedia.org/wiki/Grigori_Rasputin The forensic expert is named as Derek Pounder.
31. *Diary* (11 Jan. 1917), pp. 92-93).
32. *Diary* (12 Jan. 1917), p. 94.
33. *Ibid.*
34. *Diary* (25 Jan. 1917), p. 97.
35. *Diary* (7 Mar. 1917), p. 101.
36. *Diary* (10 Mar. 1917), p. 103.
37. *Ibid.*
38. *Diary* (11 Mar. 1917), pp. 106-107.
39. *Ibid.*, p. 107.
40. *Ibid.*
41. *Ibid.*
42. *Ibid.*, pp. 107-108.
43. *Diary* (12 Mar. 1917), p. 108. Pages missing at this point in diary.
44. *Ibid.*, p. 109.
45. *Diary* (13 Mar. 1917), p. 110.
46. *Ibid.*
47. *Diary* (14 Mar. 1917), p. 111.

48. *Diary* (24 Mar. 1917), p. 135.
49. *Diary* (15 Mar. 1917), p. 117.

CHAPTER NINE

1. Anonymous (Albert Henry Stopford): *Diary* (1919) (from 14 Mar. 1917), p. 113; (15 Mar. 1917), p. 118; (20 Mar. 1917), p. 129.
2. *Diary* (15 Mar. 1917), p. 118; (16 Mar. 1917), p. 122; (14 Mar. 1917), p. 114.
3. *Diary* (24 Mar. 1917), p. 135.
4. *Diary* (28 Mar. 1917), p. 137.
5. *Ibid.*
6. *Diary* (28 Mar. 1917), pp. 137-38.
7. *Diary* (18 Mar. 1917), p. 126.
8. *Ibid.*
9. *Ibid.*, p. 127.
10. *Diary* (1 April 1917), p. 144.
11. *Ibid.*
12. *Ibid.*, p. 145.
13. William Clarke: *Romanoff Gold: The Lost Fortunes of the Tsars* (1994/2007).
14. Anonymous: *The Fall of the Romanovs* (1918/1992).
15. *Diary* (9 April 1917), pp. 149-50.
16. *Diary* (20 April 1917), pp. 152-53.
17. *Ibid.*, p. 152.
18. *Ibid.*, p. 153.
19. *Diary* (4 April 1917), p. 156.
20. *Diary* (20 Mar. 1917), p. 130.
21. *Diary* (30 April 1917), p. 157.
22. *Diary* (2 Nov. 1915), p. 32.
23. *Diary* (5 May 1917), p. 159.
24. Serge Obolensky: *One Man in his Time* (1960), p. 158.
25. *Diary* (30 May 1916), p. 62.
26. *Ibid.*
27. *Diary* (6 June 1916), p. 63.
28. *Diary* (15 May 1917), pp. 160-61.

CHAPTER TEN

1. Prince Felix Youssoupoff: *Lost Splendour* (1953).
2. Serge Obolensky: *One Man in his Time* (1960), p. 154.
3. Ian Vorres: *The Last Great Duchess* (1964).
4. Youssoupoff (1953): *ibid.*
5. Anonymous (Albert Henry Stopford): *Diary* (1919) (from 9 April 1917), p. 150.
6. *Diary* (30 April 1917), p. 158.
7. *Ibid.*
8. Obolensky (1960): pp. 157-58.
9. *Diary* (29 June 1917), p. 167.
10. *Diary* (3 July 1917), p. 168.
11. Lady Muriel Paget's papers, Leeds University (Brotherton) Archives.
12. *Ibid.*
13. *Diary* (16 July 1917), p. 174.
14. *Ibid.*, p. 175.
15. *Diary* (19 July 1917), pp. 176-77.
16. *Diary* (25 July 1917), p. 178.
17. Youssoupoff (1953): *ibid.*

CHAPTER ELEVEN

1. The Vladimir Palace was built by Russian architect Alexander Rezanov in 1874 for Grand Duke Vladimir. It is now known as the House of Scientists, home to many scientific associations. Conducted tours are provided with an 80-page coloured booklet giving details (and photographs) of the original rooms.
2. I am indebted to Dr Idris Traylor of Texas for visiting the Palace and for asking all the right questions relating to the secret passageway.
3. Serge Obolensky: *One Man in his Time* (1960), p. 158.
4. I have based this account on two sources: Prince Nicholas of Greece [Maria Pavlovna's son-in-law]: *My Fifty Years* (1926) and a diary of HRH Princess Olga [Maria's grand-daughter]

kindly shown to me by HRH Princess Elizabeth of Yugoslavia. Later secondary sources covering the same episode include Wentworth Day: *HRH Princess Marina, Duchess of Kent* (1962); Sophia Watson: *Marina: Story of a Princess* (1994); and Suzy Menkes: *The Royal Jewels* (1985).

5. Anonymous (Albert Henry Stopford): *Diary* (1919) (from 19 August 1917), p. 189.
6. *Ibid.*, p. 186.
7. *Ibid.*, p. 187.
8. *Diary* (11 Aug. 1917), pp. 184-85.
9. *Ibid.*, p. 185.
10. *Diary* (20 Aug. 1917), p. 190.
11. *Diary* (22 Aug. 1917), p. 191.
12. *Ibid.*
13. *Diary* (26 Aug. 1917), p. 195.
14. *Ibid.*
15. *Diary* (24 Aug. 1917), p. 194.
16. *Diary* (11 Sept. 1917), p. 202.
17. *Diary* (12-13 Sept. 1917), p. 203.
18. *Diary* (13 Sept. 1917), pp. 205-206.
19. *Diary* (17 Sept. 1917), p. 208.
20. *Ibid.*
21. *Diary* (26 Aug. 1917), p. 195.
22. *Diary* (20 Sept. 1917), p. 209.
23. *Diary* (26 Sept. 1917), p. 210.
24. Mary Hughes (*neé* Stopford); Angela Price (*neé* Stopford) and Nigel Price.
25. Obolensky (1960): p. 158.
26. *Ibid.*

CHAPTER TWELVE

1. Anonymous (Albert Henry Stopford): *Diary* (1919) (from 6 Oct. 1917), p. 210.
2. Last Will and Testament of Lady Gladys de Grey, 28 April 1917, Leeds District Archives.
3. Foreign Office (FO) 395/184, United Kingdom National Archives.
4. War Office (WO) 372/19, United Kingdom National Archives.

5. FO 395/184: *ibid.*
6. Scots Guards Archives.
7. *John Bull*, 20 July 1918, British Library Newspaper Archives.
8. *Ibid.*
9. *Ibid.*
10. *John Bull*, 27 July 1918.
11. *Ibid.*
12. *Ibid.*
13. *Ibid.*
14. Duff Cooper and John Julian Norwich: *The Duff Cooper Diaries* (2006).
15. *John Bull*, 3 August 1918.
16. *Ibid.*
17. *John Bull*, 10 August 1918.
18. Home Office (HO) 140/346, UK National Archives.
19. *Ibid.*
20. *Ibid.*
21. CRIM 4/1403 and HO 140/346, UK National Archives; *John Bull*, 30 November 1918; *The Times*, 21 and 22 November 1918.

CHAPTER THIRTEEN

1. Serge Obolensky: *One Man in his Time* (1960), p. 206.
2. Obolensky (1960): *ibid.*
3. William Heinemann Publishers Archives.
4. Obolensky (1960): *ibid.*
5. Edvard Radzinsky: *The Last Tsar* (2000), pp. 354-55.
6. Foreign Office (FO/371), United Kingdom National Archives. Details in Admiralty and War Cabinet files; Vice Admiral Sir Francis Pridham: *Close of a Dynasty* (1956); Prince Roman Romanoff: *Det var et rigt hus, et lykkeligt hus* (1991).
7. Mathilde Kschessinka: *Dancing in Petersburg* (1962).
8. With thanks to HRH Princess Elizabeth of Yugoslavia and HRH Prince Michael of Kent; J. Wentworth Day: *HRH Princess Marina, Duchess of Kent* (1962).

9. Letters (1914-20) of Grand Duchess Maria Pavlovna to Alexander Ouchakoff, Paris, in the possession of HRH Princess Elizabeth of Yugoslavia.
10. I am indebted to Henry Poole, grandson of General Poole, for access to his grandfather's correspondence and diary.
11. *Ibid.*
12. *Ibid.*
13. FO/371: *ibid.*
14. Maria Pavlovna to Ouchakoff, letter, *ibid.*
15. *Ibid.*
16. *Ibid.*
17. *Ibid.*
18. *Ibid.*
19. Poole, correspondence, *ibid.*
20. Kschessinka (1960): *ibid.*
21. Ian Vorres: *The Last Grand Duchess* (1964).
22. Kschessinka (1960): *ibid.*
23. Maria Pavlovna to Ouchakoff, letter, *ibid.*
24. Kschessinka (1960): *ibid.*
25. Diary of HRH Princess Olga, grand-daughter of Maria Pavlovna, now in the possession of HRH Princess Elizabeth of Yugoslavia.
26. Letter dated 15 June 1920 from the Montreux Palace Hotel. Stopford's telegraph address was 'Stoppy, Paris'.
27. 'Contrexeville et son Histoire', pamphlet from Office de Tourisme de Contrexeville, Contrexeville; 'Voyage Travers le Temps' (France, 2000).
28. Death certificate, Mairie de Contrexeville, France, 6 September 1920.

CHAPTER FOURTEEN

1. Consuelo Vanderbilt Balsan: *The Glitter and the Gold* (1953).
2. Count Hans Veit Toerring-Jettenbach, grandson of Princess Helen of Greece and a cousin of HRH Prince Michael of Kent.

3. J. Wentworth Day: *HRH Princess Marina, Duchess of Kent* (1962).

4. Geza von Habsburg: *Fabergé-Cartier, Rivalen am Zarenhof* (Munich 2003). Contributors include Geza von Habsburg, Johan George Prince von Habsburg, Betty Jais [Cartier], Tatiana Fabergé, Alain Cartier and Alexander von Soldkoff; volume published to accompany 'Cartier Fabergé' Exhibition in Munich, 2003-04.

5. Leslie Field: *The Queen's Jewels* (1987).

6. Ileana, Princess of Rumania: *I Live Again* (1952)

7. Mathilde Kschessinka: *Dancing in Petersburg* (1960).

8. Private 64-page memorandum sent to me by Harold Lindes, Alexei Pilatsky's nephew in the United States.

9. I gratefully acknowledge the help of Count Toerring-Jeffenbach and his sister, HRH Princess Helene of Habsburg, in tracing the jewels.

10. Ileana, Princess of Rumania (1952): *ibid.*

11. *Ibid.*

12. *Ibid.*

13. J. Wentworth Day: *HRH Princess Marina, Duchess of Kent* (1962), p. 72.

14. *Ibid.*, p. 73.

15. *Ibid.*

16. Suzy Menkes: *The Royal Jewels* (1985).

17. Elizabeth Taylor: *My Love Affair With Jewelery* (2003).

18. *Daily Mail*, 16 October 1989.

19. Ileana, Princess of Rumania (1952): *ibid.*

20. Hans Nadelhoffer: *Cartier: Jewelers Extraordinary* (1984).

21. Pilatsky memorandum.

22. Serge Obolensky: *One Man in his Time* (1960).

23. Obolensky (1960): p. 23.

24. Obolensky (1960): p. 221.

CHAPTER FIFTEEN

1. Filippo Calandruccio: *Beehive. Oltre un secolo di attività turistica a Taormina* (1993).

2. Gertrude Bell Archives.

3. Pietro Nicolosi: *I Baroni di Taormina* (1959), Catania 1973. Information on the Albert Stopford rose was provided by the Association 'Rosa Gallica', France.

4. *The Letters of D. H. Lawrence* (Cambridge University Press), volume IV, February 1922.

5. *Ibid.*, volume V, 12 and 17 February 1922.

6. *Ibid.*, volume V.

7. *Ibid.*, volume III, 31 March 1920.

8. Calandruccio (1993): *ibid.*

9. *Ibid.*

10. *The Letters of D. H. Lawrence*: ibid., volume IV, December 1922, New Mexico.

11. *Ibid.*

CHAPTER SIXTEEN

1. May Bourne Strassburger Papers (Box 1 Folders 8-9), 23 February 1931. The Winterthur Library: Joseph Downs Collection of Manuscripts and Printed Ephemera, Delaware, USA. Courtesy of The Winterthur Library: Joseph Downs Collection of Manuscripts and Printed Ephmera.

2. May Bourne Strassburger Papers: *Ibid.*

3. Mary Hughes (*neé* Stopford); Angela Price (*neé* Stopford) and Nigel Price.

4. May Bourne Strassburger Papers: *Ibid.*

5. May Bourne Strassburger Papers: *Ibid.*

6. May Bourne Strassburger Papers: *Ibid.* One of the photographs of Albert Stopford that was taken by Cecil Beaton is featured in the art section in this book (on page 1).

7. May Bourne Strassburger Papers: *Ibid.*, 1930.

8. May Bourne Strassburger Papers: *Ibid.*, 3 July 1932.

9. May Bourne Strassburger Papers: *Ibid.*, 1932.

10. May Bourne Strassburger Papers: *Ibid.*, 1937.

11. May Bourne Strassburger Papers: *Ibid.*

12. Last Will and Testament of Albert Henry Stopford, dated 5 March 1930.

13. Service Centrale des Cimetiere, Paris.

14. *ibid.*

EPILOGUE

1. Serge Obolensky: *One Man in His Time* (1960), p. 206.

2. *Ibid.*

3. *Ibid.*

4. Filippo Calandruccio: *Beehive. Oltre un secolo di attività turistica a Taormina* (1993).

APPENDIX

1. William Clarke: *Romanoff Gold: The Lost Fortunes of the Tsars*.

2. Private 64-page memorandum sent to me by Harold Lindes, Alexei Pilatsky's nephew.

3. See Chapter 14 (The Jewels)

4. HSBC Group Archives, London.

5. Letters of Grand Duchess Marie (Maria) Pavlovna (Princess Elizabeth of Yugoslavia).

6. Michael Kettle: *The Allies and the Russian Collapse March 1917 to March 1918, Russia and The Allies 1917-20* (1981), vol. 1.

7. Foreign Office 371/3326; FO 371/3398, UK National Archives.

8. FO 371.

9. Home Office HO 45/11026/413565, UK National Archives.

BIBLIOGRAPHY

PUBLICATIONS

Alexander Mikhailovich, Grand Duke: *Once a Grand Duke* (New York: Farrar & Rinehart, 1932).

Anon. [Albert Henry Stopford]: *The Russian Diary of an Englishman: Petrograd, 1915-1917 (1919)* (London: William Heinemann, 1919).

Anon: *The Fall of the Romanovs* (London: Herbert Jenkins, 1992; first published in 1918).

Bainbridge, Henry C.: *Peter Carl Faberge* (London: Spring Books, 1966).

Balsam, Consuelo Vanderbilt: *The Glitter and the Gold* (London: Heinemann, 1953).

Belgion, Helen: *Titchmarsh Past and Present* (Titchmarsh: Helen Belgion, 1979).

Benson, E. F.: *As We Were* (London: Longmans, Green and Co., 1930).

Blunt, Wilfred: *Lady Muriel: Lady Muriel Paget, her husband and her philanthropic work in Central and Eastern Europe* (London: Methuen, 1962).

Buchanan, Meriel: *Ambassador's Daughter* (London: Cassell, 1958).

Buckle, Richard: *Diaghilev* (London: Weidenfeld and Nicolson/ The Orion Publishing Group, 1979).

Calandruccio, Filippo: *Beehive: oltre un secolo di attività turistica a Taormina* (Palermo: Quattrosoli, 1993).

Chavchavadze, David: *The Grand Dukes* (New York: Atlantic International Publications, 1990).

Clark, Lloyd: *World War I: An Illustrated History* (London: Bounty Books, 2004).

Clarke, William: *Romanoff Gold: The Lost Fortunes of the Tsars* (Gloucestershire: Sutton Publishing, 2007); originally published in 1994 by Weidenfeld & Nicolson.

Cook, Andrew: *To Kill Rasputin: The Life and Death of Grigori Rasputin* (London: Tempus, 2005).

Cooper, Diana: *The Rainbow Comes and Goes* (London: R. Hart-Davis, 1959).

Cooper, Duff and John Julian Norwich (ed): *The Duff Cooper Diaries: 1915-1951* (London: Weidenfeld and Nicolson/The Orion Publishing Group, 2006).

Day, J. Wentworth: *HRH Princess Marina, Duchess of Kent* (London: Robert Hale, 1962).

Dobson, Christopher: *Prince Felix Yusupov* (London: Harrap, 1989).

Field, Leslie: *The Queen's Jewels* (New York: Harry N. Abrams, 1987).

Fitzpatrick, Sheila: *The Russian Revolution* (Oxford University Press, 2008) (third edition).

Gattey, Charles Neilson: *Queens of Song* (London: Barrie and Jenkins, 1979).

Harmer, Michael: *The Forgotten Hospital* (Chichester: Springwood, 1982).

House of Scientists. Palace of Grand Duke Vladimir (St Petersburg, 2003), in Russian and English.

Hyde, H. Montgomery: *Oscar Wilde* (London: Eyre Methuen, 1976).

Hyman, Alan: *The Rise and Fall of Horatio Bottomley* (London: Cassell, 1972).

Ileana, Princess of Rumania: *I Live Again* (London: Gollancz, 1952).

The Illustrated London News (1912-17) (London: The Illustrated London News and Sketch Limited).

Karsavina, Tamara: *Theatre Street* (London: William Heinemann, 1930).

Kettle, Michael: *The Allies and the Russian Collapse, March 1917 to March 1918, Russia and the Allies* (London: Deutsch, 1981), volume 1.

Kettle, Michael: *Road to Intervention: March to November 1918, Russia and the Allies* (London: Deutsch, 1981), volume 2.

Kschessinka, Mathilde: *Dancing in Petersburg* (London: The Orion Publishing Group, 1960).

Marie Louise, Princess: *My Memories of Six Reigns* (London: Evans Brothers, 1957).

Marie Pavlovna [Jnr], Grand Duchess of Russia: *Education of a Princess: A Memoir* (London/New York: The Viking Press, 1931) (translated from French and Russian under editorial supervision of Russell Lord).

Melba, Nellie: *Melodies and Memories* (London: Thornton Butterworth, 1925).

Menkes, Suzy: *The Royal Jewels* (London: Grafton Books, 1985).

Nadelhoffer, Hans: *Cartier: Jewelers Extraordinary* (London: Thames & Hudson Ltd, 1984).

Nicholas and Alexandra: The Last Tsar and Tsarina (Edinburgh:

NMS Enterprises Limited – Publishing, 2005), National Museums Scotland/State Hermitage Museum, exhib. catalogue.

Nicholas of Greece (Prince of Denmark): *My Fifty Years* (London: Hutchison & Co., 1926).

Nicolosi, Pietro: *I Baroni di Taormina, Palermo fin de siecle*, Series: Citta, fatti, e figure; 11 (Milano: Mursia Ed., 1979).

Nicolson, Juliet: *The Perfect Summer: England 1911, Just Before the Storm* (London: Grove Press, 2007).

Obolensky, Serge: *One Man in His Time* (London: Hutchinson, 1960/The Random House Group Ltd).

Our King and Queen: A Pictorial Record (ed. J. A. Hammerton) (London: The Educational Book Co. Limited, n.d.), volumes 1 and 2.

Perry, John Curtis and Constantine Pleshakov: *The Flight of the Romanovs: A Family Saga* (New York: Basic Books, 1999).

Pipes, Richard: *The Russian Revolution, 1899-1919* (London: Harvill, 1990/The Random House Group Ltd).

Pridham, Vice Admiral Sir Francis: *Close of a Dynasty* (London: Allan Wingate, 1956).

Radzinsky, Edvard: *The Last Tsar* (London: Arrow Books, 1993).

Radzinsky, Edvard: *The Rasputin File* (orig. published in the US by Doubleday, 2000).

Reynolds, M. E.: *Memories of John Galsworthy* (London: Robert Hale, 1936).

Robottom, John: *Modern Russia* (London: Longman, 1972) (second edition).

Romanoff, Prince Roman: *Det var et rigt hus, et lykkeligt hus; På dansk ved Wera Friis Kelstrup* (Copenhagen: Gyldendals Bogklubber, 1991).

Rudoe, Julie: *Cartier: 1900-1939* (New York: Harry N. Abrams, 1997).

Snowman, A. Kenneth: *Carl Fabergé: Goldsmith to the Imperial Court of Russia* (London: Debretts Peerage, 1980).

Taylor, Elizabeth: *My Love Affair with Jewelery* (London: Simon & Schuster, 2003).

Tuchman, Barbara W.: *The Guns of August – August 1914* (London: Constable, 1962).

Vilinbakhov, George (*et al.*): *Nicholas and Alexandra: The Last Imperial Family of Tsarist Russia* (London/New York: Booth-Clibborn Editions/Harry N. Abrams Inc., 1998) from the State Hermitage Museum/ State Archive of the Russian Federation), exhibition catalogue.

von Habsburg, Geza and Avon Solodkoff: *Faberge: Court Jeweller to the Tsar* (London: Studio Vista/Christie's, 1979).

von Habsburg, Geza: *Fabergé/ Cartier, Rivalen am Zarenhof* (Munich: Hirmer Verlag, 2003). Contributors include Geza von Habsburg, Johan George Prince von Habsburg, Betty Jais (Cartier), Tatiana Fabergé, Alain Cartier and Alexander von Soldkoff. Published to accompany *Cartier Fabergé* exhibition in Munich, 2003-04.

Vorres, Ian: *The Last Grand Duchess* (London: Hutchinson, 1964).

The War Illustrated album deluxe (ed. J. A. Hammerton) (London: The Amalgamated Press Ltd, 1915 and 1916), volume I (*The First Phase*), volume II (*The Winter Campaign*), volume IV (*The Summer Campaign 1915*), volume V (*The Winter Campaign 1915-16*).

Watson, Sophia: *Marina: The Story of a Princess* (London: Weidenfeld and Nicolson, 1994).

Williams, Mrs Hwfa: *It Was Such Fun* (London: Hutchinson & Co., 1935).

Youssoupoff, Prince Felix: *Rasputin; His Malignant Influence and his Assassination* (London: Jonathan Cape, 1934).

Youssoupoff, Prince Felix: *Lost Splendour* (London: Jonathan Cape, 1953).

PERIODICALS

– *Daily Mail*
– *Daily Mirror*
– *The Dancing Times*
– *John Bull* (British Library Newspaper Archives)
– *New York Times*
– *The Observer*
– *The Tatler*
– *The Times* (London)

'Contrexeville et son Histoire', a pamphlet available from the Office de Tourisme de Contrexeville, Contrexeville; 'Voyage Travers le Temps' (France, 2000).

Royal Opera House Collections: Charles Neilson Gattey: 'Lady de Grey and the Garden's Golden Age', in *About the House* (London: The Friends of Covent Garden, Spring 1992).

'Titchmarsh', booklet, Northamptonshire Record Office.

CORRESPONDENCE, DIARIES AND PRIVATE PAPERS

Gabriel Anstruc Papers, New York Public Library for the Performing Arts, Dance Division, Lincoln Center, New York.

Lady Constance Gladys, Marchioness of Ripon, Last Will and Testament, dated 28 April 1917, Leeds District Archives, Sheepscar, Leeds.

Frank C. Cousins Collection: correspondence from Frank Cousins to his sister, Scots Guards Archive, Wellington Barracks, London.

Eric Hamilton, Private Memoir of (from University College Archives, Oxford), unpublished.

Gretchen Haskins: a private memorandum.

D. H. Lawrence: Extracts from *The Letters of D. H. Lawrence*, vols III, IV and V (Pollinger Limited, The Estate of Frieda

Lawrence Ravagli and Cambridge University Press, 1979, 1981, 1984, 1987, 1989, 1991, 1993).

Maria Pavlovna, Grand Duchess: letters to Alexander Ouchakoff in Paris (1914-1920); letter dated 15 June 1920 from Maria Pavlovna at Monteux Palace Hotel to Albert Stopford (source: HRH Princess Elizabeth of Yugoslavia).

HRH Princess Olga [Maria Pavlovna's grand-daughter]: Princess Olga's diary (source: HRH Princess Elizabeth of Yugoslavia).

Lady Muriel Paget Papers. Leeds Russian Archive MS.1405, Leeds University Library.

Alexei Pilatsky: a 64-page memorandum from Harold Lindes (nephew of Alexei Pilatsky) to the author.

General Frederick Poole: correspondence and diary of General Poole.

Frances Stopford to Canon Luckock: correspondence from F. Stopford to Luckock, dated 2 April 1912 [328p/23/1] and 18 August 1912 [328p/23/2] from Northamptonshire Record Office.

May Bourne Strassburger Papers (Box 1 Folders 8-9), The Winterthur Library: Joseph Downs Collection of Manuscripts and Printed Ephemera, Delaware, USA.

State Archives of the Russian Federation, Moscow, Russia: Grand Duchess Maria Pavlovna Sr. Fond 655.

Reverend Frederick Manners Stopford, Last Will and Testament, Family Records Centre (Births, Marriages, Deaths Certificates), Myddleton Street, London.

Albert Henry Stopford, Last Will and Testament, dated 5 March 1930, General Register Office (UK Government Home Office www.gro.gov.uk).

DOCUMENTARY

BBC Two: Timewatch Documentary, *Who Killed Rasputin?*, 1 October 2004.

PAPERS AND ARCHIVES

– *Burke's Peerage*
– Censuses of 1871, 1881, and 1891
– Crawford's Clerical Records
– *Debrett's*
– HSBC Group Archives
– Heinemann Archives
– Lambeth Palace Archives

Mairie de Contrexeville, France: Death certificate of Maria Pavlovna, dated 6 September 1920.

The National Archives, Kew:

CRIM 4/1403	FO 371
FO 371/3326	FO 371/3398
FO 395/184	HO 140/346
HO 45/11026/413565	
WO 339/55793	WO 372/19

www.nationalarchives.gov.uk

– Royal Kalendar
– Service Centrale des Cimitiere, Paris.
– State Archives of the Russian Federation, Moscow, Russia.
– Wartski's Archives, Grafton Street, London: Fabergé accounts, 1900s.

INTERVIEWEES AND FURTHER ASSISTANCE

Archivist, University College, Oxford

HRH Princess Elizabeth of Yugoslavia, grand-daughter of Princess Helen of Greece

Count Hans Veit Toerring-Jettenbach, grandson of Princess Helen of Greece and a cousin of HRH Prince Michael of Kent.

HRH Princess Helene of Habsburg, grand-daughter of Princess Helen of Greece.

Mary Hughes (*neé* Stopford)

NMS Photography

HRH Prince Michael of Kent, grandson of Princess Helen of Greece.

Giovanni Panarello

Angela Price (*neé* Stopford) and and Nigel Price

INTERNET RESEARCH

wikipedia

http://en.wikipedia.org/wiki/Lenin

http://en.wikipedia.org/wiki/Lavr_Kornilov

http://en.wikipedia.org/wiki/Marie_of Mecklenburg-Schwerin

http://en.wikipedia.org/wiki/Serge_Obolensky

INDEX